TOGETHER FOREVER

An Invitation to be Physically Immortal

Charles Paul Brown

BernaDeane

James Russell Strole

The Pythagorean Press
Sydney & Auckland

We dedicate this book...

☆ to all people on this planet who want to live free from the sentence of death!

☆ to those who have hungered to live beyond all limitations, yearning for a quality of life on this planet greater than any humanity has yet known.

☆ to all those who refuse to be stifled by public opinion in their continuing human expansion and adventure.

☆ to those people who are letting go of age-old belief systems that have helped create division and conflict within humankind.

☆ to all who are eager to put an end to conflict and war, who want to see a confluence of people throughout the world fused in creating a safe place to be totally alive.

☆ to those we haven't reached yet, but for whom our meeting is inevitable.

☆ to all people who have made a commitment to be together forever—we will create heaven on earth and a world without end!

☆ last, but not least, to all the people who have contributed directly or indirectly to the publication of this book. We celebrate with you forever. Thank you for being with us!

Acknowledgments

We want to thank a number of people who helped make this book a reality.

Donald Leon and Lynne Ericksson were instrumental in conveying their vision for the book, suggesting topics to be covered, and inspiring us to our fullest expressions on these subjects.

Robin Beaudette was primarily responsible for the initial transcription of the text from our spoken expressions, with help from Marla and Ronda Sargent. Cheryl Ambrose, Jenny McFeely and Jon Ward all proofread the manuscript.

We especially wanted the book to include some visual images that would complement the text, and the photography of Lynne Ericksson, Anil Chanrai and Fred Stevens has served this purpose beautifully. The wonderful cover design was the product of Ed Powers.

Marlena Wilson proved invaluable in the process of getting the book printed.

Our special thanks go to Treva La Munyon, whose guiding hand helped steer this project, like so many others, to a successful completion.

Finally, we want to thank Herb Bowie, who had the job of editing our verbal expressions into written form, and doing the layout for the book. Without his dedication and persistence, this book would never have achieved the form you see it in today.

Contents

A New Kind of Courage

by Herb Bowie

I want to acknowledge the authors of this book for their aliveness, their passion and, perhaps most of all, their courage.

We are used to thinking of courage in terms of a person's willingness to lay down his life, usually for a cause or a country. To be truly brave, we say, one must be willing to die, to make the ultimate sacrifice, to give up one's life.

But Charles Paul, Bernadeane and James Russell require us to define courage in new terms. Death, after all, is a proven thing, as predictable as the ticking of a clock, as certain as taxes. To be willing to die is to do no more than our ancestors have done, without fail, for generation after generation. Death, at this point, can hardly be called a risky proposition. On the contrary, it is a proven quantity, tried and true, never known to fail. As the life insurance companies will tell you, death is a safe investment.

Most people think their biggest fear is death. I will tell you a secret, though: there is something else that they are more afraid of—total aliveness!

What do I mean by total aliveness? Certainly not the slow death that so many people experience. I mean a life of constant growth, continual expansion, a life of intimacy, where our greatest desire is to plunge ever deeper with each other. I mean a life without limits, without end.

Why should that frighten us? Because it puts us at odds with death. After all, for those who have already acquiesced to death, who have already thrown in the towel, the worst is over—there is nothing more to lose, nothing left to fear.

Charles Paul, Bernadeane and James are telling us that life is richer and more exciting than we have ever dreamed!

The alternative is to not give in, to deny death, which we have been programmed to believe is impossible.

How can we deny death? We can expect no

help from our philosophies, our metaphysics, or our gods. To live free of death means we have to rely on ourselves, on our own passion, on our own aliveness, and on each other. We have to be willing to renounce all our comforting beliefs in abstract principles, and live each moment fully as flesh and blood and bone.

Now this is a life worth living! One that requires a new level of courage, beyond anything humanity has yet known.

Charles Paul, Bernadeane and James are spearheading this new life. They give all of themselves, to each other, and to those around them. They hold nothing back.

They are telling us that life is richer and more exciting than we have ever dreamed. They are saying that we are enough for each other, that we are all we need, that we will never tire of each other. They tell all who will hear that life is worth living...

Forever!

Charles Paul, Bernadeane and James are living this life, a life that is just beginning: I don't know about you, but I'm ready to live it with them.

The End of the Path

by Dr. Donald E. Leon, J.D., Ph.D.

A foreword to this very unusual and important book must start with an introduction to Charles Paul, Bernadeane and James Russell, ("CBJ," as they are affectionately called). I first met these three in 1985 when I moved from Los Angeles, California to Scottsdale, Arizona. *WOW!* What an experience! These three amazing people, along with a large group of others who had gathered from all over the United States to be with them, were actually *living* physical immortality. At that time it had been twenty-five years since Charles and Bernadeane had first known that death of the physical body was not their way. James joined them in this cellular realization a few years later, and since then the three of them have been sharing their new reality around the world with all people.

What CBJ express is revolutionary. They are destroying the very foundations of the world's belief systems. They are not working at becoming physically immortal. They do not teach a new philosophy about physical immortality. Nor are they starting a new religion. They actually *are* physically immortal, a new species. They have experienced a basic change at the cellular, biological level of their bodies.

> ## What CBJ express is revolutionary. They are destroying the very foundations of the world's belief systems.

I find them to have an integrity that is greater than any I have ever known. They constantly risk losing everything by always being real, never being political. They never sell out to either public or private opinion. This makes them the most reliable, most available, most trustworthy people in the world.

CBJ are the first people to go through this cellular, biological transformation. I stress the physicality of their change in order to distinguish them from others who call themselves "immortalists," or who say they are physically immortal. Some immortalists define immortality to mean the eternal life of one's essence. Others believe that with enough training and practices they will learn how to "take their body with them" when they die.

Charles Paul, Bernadeane and James Russell are bringing the world a totally different reality. They know that all of the cleansings, purifications, meditations, rituals, diets and exercises will never assure physical immortality. Only the cellular connection created between people who have awakened in their bodies to this new reality will stop death on this planet. So CBJ travel the world sounding a call for people to wake up to who they really are—a new species. They know that there is a biological attraction between those people who will never leave each other by dying—or through any other means. This cellular agreement permits a depth of intimacy never before available. They support each immortal person to be all they can be. They support realness. No one can ever be "too much" for them. They are creating a way of life for people of all nations that previously was only a dream.

CBJ have discovered that it is possible and even exciting to live outside of all belief systems: even the universal belief, common to all the cultures on the planet, that "death is inevitable." This foundation block, or meta-belief, is at the base of all belief systems. How belief systems create reality for each person is worth looking at more closely. However, before I go into this area more deeply, I would like to share some of my background with you.

I practiced law in the Los Angeles area for seventeen years. My practice was mostly in the area of Entertainment Law, Business and Real Estate, and Domestic Relations. During this exciting and creative legal career, however, I was totally asleep! I was living out my life "script" in blissful ignorance. One day I discovered I had socialized myself into a full-blown alcoholic! At that point I stopped my legal career and began a twenty-five year journey into psychology and metaphysics, specializing in belief systems and thinking structures. For the first time I became aware that I was responsible for all my experiences and relationships.

This journey led me to AA (Alcoholics Anonymous), then to Overeaters Anonymous. I decided to do extensive studying in the field of psychology. I earned a Master's degree in Marriage, Family and Child Counseling and then a Ph.D. in Clinical Psychology. I opened a counseling and psychotherapy practice in Beverly Hills and established a low-cost psychology clinic. I became clinically certified in the specialty of Transactional Analysis (T.A.), and co-founded the T.A. Training Institute of Beverly Hills. I also co-directed the Psychology and Counseling Training Center in Southern California and became an Adjunct Professor of Psychology at the Goddard International Colleges.

All of my work in the psychological field was done simultaneously with my explorations into alternative belief systems. I trained for years in the Church of Religious Science, a metaphysical church, and worked extensively with a native American Indian Shaman. All of these studies led me into "channeling" and I became a medium for the so-called Ascended Masters. I studied and then taught *A Course in Miracles* and finally became a disciple of an Eastern Guru. During these years I co-created a foundation, called Beliefs, Inc., dedicated to researching and teaching belief systems and thinking structures.

As a result of all this training, teaching and experience, I became very intimate with the fact that each person creates their future reality by first being exposed to a series or network of programmings, and then making early childhood decisions based on either complying with or rebelling against these programs.

> *These decisions result in an integrated system of beliefs, which then determine one's lifetime reality.*

These decisions result in an integrated system of beliefs, which then determine one's lifetime reality. These decisions can be changed and belief systems altered. However, most people are not aware that they have created their own reality and never wake up to who they really are.

As a T.A. therapist and trainer, I discovered early in my career that once people make their early decisions and create their belief systems, they integrate them in a "Life Script." This Life Script then determines the basic flow of their lives, including all the major elements of their experience of reality. Once this Life Script is written, it is forgotten by the conscious mind and becomes very resistant to change. Beliefs are connected in such a way as to reinforce each other. Many belief systems become interlocked, reinforcing each other and creating "Meta-Beliefs." Experiences are then used to prove the "truth" of

One of the most fundamental of early childhood decisions is the decision of how and when to die.

these beliefs and all evidence to the contrary is discounted, disbelieved and ignored. Thus reality continues to match our expectations both consciously and unconsciously.

When I had my psychotherapy practice, people came for treatment who really wanted to change their lives. I would aid them in discerning their programming, early decisions and life script. In order to make rapid changes it is necessary to find the meta-beliefs, or foundation stones upon which all of the others are based. Once found and changed, all of the subsidiary beliefs and decisions automatically crumble. A person becomes able to redecide and reincorporate a new series of belief systems and thus change their life realities.

One of the most fundamental of early childhood decisions, and one that is common to all people, is the decision of how and when to die. The following are examples of how early programming leads to childhood decisions around death that are lived out rather than changed.

When Bill was growing up he was told by his family that he was just like his uncle Fred. Fred became his idol. He dreamed of growing up and someday becoming just like his uncle, but then Fred died in an auto accident at age thirty-two. Bill became very depressed but recovered. Later at age thirty-one Bill also had a fatal accident.

Another illustration is the case of Sally. As a young child she was told over and over how much her mother had done for her, how her mother was sacrificing her whole life for her daughter and how Sally "owed" her. After Sally's father died she lived with and took care of her aging mother. After many years her mother finally died of cancer at age seventy-one. Sally then led a normal life until she contracted the same type of cancer as her mother and died at the age of seventy-two.

I had great success over the years in aiding clients to redecide their Life Scripts, including the parts concerning their deaths. However, since the meta-belief that physical death was inevitable never changed, the best I could do was to facilitate a new decision to die at an older age or from less painful causes. After all, we all "knew" that everyone had to physically die. So, of course, everyone died.

This seemed to be as far as I could go: as long as death was inevitable, there was no possibility of total freedom. I could change and aid others to change some of the beliefs that rested upon this one immutable foundation. I could guide them to afterlives, past lives, Gods, Masters, universal mind, heavens and hells and an infinite number of other creations to make death acceptable and easier to bear. But true freedom and total change eluded me.

Then I experienced the greatest change of my life—I met CBJ. They had actually undone the foundation stone of all belief systems. Physical death was no longer inevitable. Even more important, they had not substituted the belief in physical immortality as a new meta-belief. CBJ had actually discovered that when the old, universal belief is removed it is possible to live free of all beliefs!

CBJ found they needed other immortals in cellular agreement with them, not a new system of beliefs. This shift is truly brand new. CBJ are the first to go beyond physical death and enlightenment to true freedom.

Because the connection between physical immortals is biological, rather than mental, we can never leave each other. So CBJ have brought the end to separation. They will never leave me, not even by dying, and now I too have experienced an irreversible change. I too am physically immortal and will never leave them.

CBJ found they needed other immortals in cellular agreement with them, not a new system of beliefs.

This is CBJ's first book. After thirty years of living and sharing physical immortality with the world they have finally put some of their fundamental "knowing" into a wonderful, easily assimilated work. However, in reading it, don't bother to look for formulas. There aren't any. CBJ do, however, give you all you need to know in order to decide if physical immortality is for you. They have created a biological shift, a genetic shift, that is available to all.

One Body

by Lynne Ericksson, M.A.

My primary medium of expression is photography, not words. The pictures of
mine that appear later in this book
speak the loudest about who Charles Paul, Bernadeane and James Russell are and what we are
doing together around the world. I encourage you
to take the time with each photograph to feel the
people and their connection to each other. Let each
image guide you deeply into Charles, Bernadeane
and James so that you can know for yourself, from
inside your body, the depth of their integrity, the
intensity of their concern for each person and their
total commitment to creating a new world. They
are awakening people in all countries to the fact
that there is a new species of humans evolving
right now inside every cell in the body. As a new

species, we are vibrant and alive, ageless and deathless, and totally connected to each other cellularly.

These images were created around the globe during meetings and playtime, sightseeing trips and in-depth intense sharings. Many of our communications happen through interpreters because of language differences. But, as you can see, the language of the body is stronger. Being "together forever" speaks louder than words and our biological connection is always stronger than any verbal connection has ever been. All of these people feel their interlinking with each other very deeply regardless of their location or whether they have met each other yet or not. This is the "cellular connection" happening in our physical bodies as we focus with Charles, Bernadeane and James throughout the world.

The purpose of this book is to give you a feeling of what this new species is all about, as well as a taste of this amazing "cellular connection" I've referred to. Of course, since this new state of being is happening physically, you will need to connect with CBJ and the people around the world personally. Reading about it can only spark your desire to experience firsthand what we are all sharing together with Charles, Bernadeane and James. I know that, for myself, I have been preparing my whole life for this moment, for these people. I know no other experience as fulfilling and joyous as seeing people "wake up" to being really alive—releasing their creativity, going beyond the petty self-centeredness that has been programmed by a world of survival and greed, and really caring for each other. As the old programs drop away from lack of relevance, the true beauty and individuality of each person is quickly coming to expression. And without the robot-like surface manners we have all been culturally encoded with, each one is delightful in their total unique-ness. No one can be replaced by anyone else because each person has a different quality, a new perspective, a special place in the "one body" that we are together.

> *Each person has a special place in the "one body" that we are together.*

I enjoy fantasizing about the future world we can create together when we are all beyond competition and limitations, combining our unique creativities in the direction of mutual pleasure, expansion and true caring for each other. With the potential of our brains released, our prosperity redirected and our purposes aligned, the possibilities of our co-creations are totally unlimited, formed only by the richness of our imaginations and the depth of our commitment to one another.

So I invite you to sit back, relax and let the words of Charles, Bernadeane and James stimulate your cells, while the images of the "cellular connection" they are bringing to everyone in the world tickle your most intimate longings for the actual experience of "one body" so

> *I invite you to sit back, relax and let the words of Charles, Bernadeane and James stimulate your cells.*

long promised. Then you only need to check where CBJ are going to be next and join us. I look forward to meeting you there. Please tell me who you are and how this book has changed your life.

Introduction

This book has been written as the result of a growing awareness in all three of us—Charles Paul, Bernadeane and James Russell—that there are people scattered all over the country, and all over the world, who are experiencing a deep hunger for physical immortality. Although we have been speaking and writing on this subject for thirty years, and our travels have taken us all over the globe, it seems the more appearances we make, and the more people we contact, the more keenly we become aware of those we have not yet been able to reach. So we hope that this book will go to places we have not yet seen, and be read by those who might otherwise never hear of us: we want no cry to go unanswered.

The format of this book is unusual, and requires some explanation. When it comes to the core of our feelings about immortality, we three speak as one body; at the same time, each of us is very different from the other two and we each have our own unique ways of expressing ourselves. In writing this book, then, we sought a format that would allow us to come forth as distinct individuals, and yet do so without obscuring our common goals and purpose.

The result is that we will speak to you in a number of different voices throughout this book: our three individual ones, and a common voice for sections that we have jointly authored. The central portion of each chapter will be in the common voice, with one or more individual expressions at the beginning and/or the end. Individual expressions will appear in italics, and expressions in the common voice will not be italicized.

A subject as vast as physical immortality cannot be treated comprehensively in a single volume. As a matter of fact, it cannot be covered completely in any number of volumes—as you will see once you begin reading, physical immortality is everything that we are, and since we are without limits, we will be constantly exploring new frontiers in physical immortality.

What we have tried to do in this book, then, is to give you an appreciation of the core of what physical immortality is to us, today. This book cannot make you physically immortal: that seed is already present within you. Our goal

The seed of physical immortality is already present within you.

for this book is to awaken you to that reality, to stir that immortal seed until it bursts forth, takes root, and begins to grow.

1

Physical Immortality

Humankind has always had some innate sense of being eternal. The difference in being physically immortal is that we have the ability to continuously renew, regenerate, restructure, and recreate our physical bodies so that we can remain here forever. As immortals, we have the ability to acclimate ourselves to any situation, to prevent ourselves from being subject to aging and death.

In most religions, there is the feeling that someday we will return to an immortal state. This is why so many religions have created the image of the heaven, or the afterlife. There is a promise of paradise after death, because man cannot come to grips with ending death now.

Many religions also teach that man will be physically immortal right here on the planet, and that heaven will be right here on earth, after the earth goes through a cleansing and purification. But until man experiences the vision of the purpose for ending death—the resulting quality of life that could be produced here on the planet—immortality will always be put off into the future, and will never actually come to pass.

Physical immortality is about you and me being able to live on this planet and not lose our physical bodies. This is not to be confused with eternal life, or anything concerning the spirit world. We're talking about our physical body being able to constantly rejuvenate itself, renew itself and not go into the grave.

Death is not natural, even though it has been the norm up until this time. Death has been imposed upon the body. Once this imposition is removed, the body has the ability to function in its true natural state, which is constant rejuvenation.

None of us can be immortal as lone identities, however. Many people have strived for this, and it has never been accomplished. We contain the power within ourselves to keep each other's lives, to stir that which has never been stirred before in each other's bodies, to stimulate the immortal potential that is there, the eternal flame. This flame exists already in the cells and atoms of our bodies. It is the stirring of one another's bodies, what we call the quickening of one another, that fans that flame and causes it to spread until it consumes the whole body.

This is why intimacy is an integral part of physical immortality. Immortality is the greatest state of intimacy, the deepest intimacy that anyone has had or will have on this planet. Immortality requires us to put aside our egos, our tendencies to separate from one another, all of our divisions

> *It is the fusion with one another that keeps our lives.*

from one another. We have to put all of that aside to really fuse with one another, because it is the fusion that keeps our lives. It is our fusion that releases the necessary energy of life from our cells, releases it through the body and makes us not only want to live forever, but causes the reactions in the body that can heal the scars of death. It is the suppression of this life energy that kills our bodies, that creates disease, and that creates all of the divisions from one another on this planet.

This life energy can preserve us from all forms of death, even accidents. We are not accidents on our way to happen. We determine everything that's going to happen to us. If someone has an accident, that is because there is some place in their own body, that they have created, that has left room for that accident to happen. This is true even for children, although children's accidents are usually just reflections of their parents' struggles.

When we are awake cellularly in our bodies, there is an alertness, there is an awareness, that intuitively keeps us from putting ourselves in a life-threatening situation. Because we have taken on a physical reality in which we are not subject to death, we draw to us only that which is our immortal living.

We are not leaving any room for death to happen by accident, by what is called a natural death or by any other way of dying. We're closing all of the doors of death.

T he only thing that can release this life energy is giving ourselves 100% to each other! Until we do that, there will never be peace on this planet, there will never be the prosperity that all humankind dreams of, much less the ending of death. We must fuse and give ourselves 100% to each other in that nourishment and that love. That is the immortal love that ends death.

It's so important to recognize what this can really mean. Physical immortality will totally transform the quality of our existence here on this planet.

Man, by accepting that death is inevitable, that he is locked into a life and death cycle, has made himself a prisoner of time. This view prevents us from seeing the truth, that time must end individually within our physical bodies. As this change transpires, and we envision the quality of living associated with a deathless society, there is the feeling that we really can create heaven on Earth, that nations can cease to war with one another, that a paradise on Earth is possible.

Physical immortality will totally transform the quality of our existence here on this planet.

All this may seem impossible to the mind that has been programmed that death is inevitable. However, the quality of life that humanity cries out for on the planet cannot possibly come forth, until we look at the core of the problem, which is the acceptance of death, the belief that death is inevitable. This is why physical immortality is so important to humanity.

Physical immortality is not a new philosophy. We're not just bringing another philosophy to the planet. Immortality is you, it is me. What is so unique about physical immortality is that what we are offering to the world is one another. That is a very rich resource that has never been totally tapped.

Immortality is more than what we do, or what we believe: it is who we are. The experience of immortal life may change our beliefs, and our actions, but our awakening to who we are must come first.

☆ ☆ ☆ ☆ ☆

*P*hysical immortality, to me, is me. It's every cell and every fiber of me. That's what I am. Physical immortality is Bernadeane. In other words, it's not a belief system to me. It's not something floating out there in the atmosphere, somewhere that I'm going to eventually get a hold of and grasp. It's not something that I'm getting from somebody else. It's what I am. Physical immortality is who I am. That

Physical immortality is every cell and fibre of me.

means that Bernadeane has no end, I'm endless. It means that I have no death in me. I can't find death within my flesh at all. To me, that's what physical immortality is all about. Physical immortality is Bernadeane walking the face of the Earth, here to stay, here to come in contact with other people who are physically immortal.

We always have been and always will be immortal. The only thing that is happening with us today is that we're waking up, we're finding our true identity. That's what happened to me. I woke up.

My awakening came by way of somebody else. Physical immortality did not come to me from someone else, it was me from the start. But my awakening to being physically immortal did come from another person, and I'm very grateful for that.

To me that's the reality of physical immortality, that by way of one another we are awakening today to who we really are.

And in that, all of our purposes and goals have taken on a different form. Prior to our awakening to who we really are, we were death oriented. We were programmed and patterned unto dying. We were born to die and that's all we knew. But when I had the initial awakening that I had no death in me, that changed my whole concept of everyday living. I wasn't looking forward to death sometime. Everything took on a different look to me.

— Bernadeane

2

A Cellular Awakening

We feel that the immortal cells of the body have experienced a deep sleep, a sleep of death. As a person hears of immortality, there is a responding vibration in the cells. There is a language of the body that is apart from the conscious, learned awareness or intelligence. I am speaking of an intelligence of the body on a cellular level. The conscious mind may say it doesn't understand, but the cells respond, and a chemical action and reaction begins to take place. There is, somewhere, a deep remembrance that, "Yes, I was born to be immortal. I was not born to die." That is the cellular awakening.

This experience bypasses the programmed mind that would seem to feel that it is ruler of the body because it knows so much. We're passing that intellect of so called truth, and going to the core of the body itself and *awakening the cells of the body. The cells respond by releasing an immortal intelligence, totally dethroning the conscious awareness of death.*

When there begins to be that touch on a cellular level, it begins to touch the nervous system, because everything is a chemical action/reaction that goes on within the physical body. The cells begin to open, the immortal cells begin to change, and they begin to send forth an immortal intelligence throughout the body.

A metamorphosis is taking place.

An upheaval takes place and one may begin to experience emotions they've never experienced before.

A metamorphosis is taking place. There is the change from a mortal intelligence to an immortal intelligence, and for a time those two worlds are conflicting, they are colliding right within the physical body. This conflict may be so strong that bodies may even feel they are experiencing a nervous breakdown. And they are! The old, mortal, nervous system is collapsing, and a new one is taking its place that will no longer be affected by the power of death.

The upheaval may be tremendous, but we're not to be afraid of these feelings and emotions as the change takes place. Unless there is a cellular response, and unless the nervous system is affected, there is no cellular awakening. As long as the reception of immortality is limited to a mental level, then it is nothing but taking notes. This awakening may be frightening, but the only alternative is to go back to sleep, to become numb all over, and to continue with the walking dead.

— Charles Paul

☆ ☆ ☆ ☆ ☆

There is no specific situation that triggers a cellular experience. It could be when you're riding your bike down the street and suddenly an idea becomes flesh. It passes beyond a mental concept and you start feeling the idea from the core of your body. You feel the aliveness of it, rather than it just being a thought.

A cellular experience could take place when you are with a group of people and there is an inspiration taking place at that moment. It could be when somebody is speaking and throughout the audience, something is stirred which goes beyond the mind, involving the intelligence of the whole body.

It could come about by means of an expression to a particular individual. That person could be penetrated by the passion of other bodies. That person realizes, then, he is not being criticized, but is receiving a deep love.

A cellular experience could happen by way of a dream at night. You could be sleeping, and your whole body feels the awakening and you stir from your sleep and you can feel a quaking taking place.

A cellular experience doesn't always feel good. Sometimes a cellular awakening is very uncomfortable, because it shakes up your whole system.

It can be very disturbing, because of the newness and apparent strangeness of it. It can feel like an earthquake is happening within your own form.

A cellular experience is not the same for every person, however. One may be sitting somewhere just reveling in the awakening that's taking place, while another right next to them might be feeling horrible about it. In the long run, though, feeling uncomfortable is just as good as feeling comfortable. What's important is the response of the flesh.

In order to have a cellular experience, one must be open to a new depth of feeling throughout the body. This is difficult for many people, since our society has programmed us to focus our consciousness in our minds, and has taught us not to trust our bodies. This training has resulted in a deep sleep in our cells, a sleep that is often hard to overcome.

W e have often taught each other to sleep the sleep of death. We have anesthetized ourselves from our real in-depth feelings for one another. As a result, we inflict abuse on each other in the name of survival. It comes out over money, and many other things that are trivial and shallow compared to what we really need to be to each other. It's like a sleep that's there in the body.

It starts when a child is born, right from the beginning. We begin to protect the child from really feeling. We hide our real emotions from each other. We don't come out and tell each other when we are hurt. We teach our children not to communicate, not to express their feelings.

When there is something going on emotionally between parents, they many times say, "Well, let's not talk about that in front of Johnny." So, Johnny feels something in his body that he doesn't understand, because it hasn't been explained to him. He can't comprehend all the

> *As immortals, we can no longer "put the lid" on each other or ourselves.*

meaning that is there, so all he knows is to cram it inside himself, because he's feeling so much that he doesn't understand. So, there are all of these hidden emotions going on all the time.

Another example of this programming is the way most parents express their frustration with their children's behavior. If they are angry at their children, or their children are angry, the easiest way to handle it has been to spank them. This has been one of parents' biggest cop-outs, because it has been a total avoidance of the parent's responsibility, and of the child's feelings. The parents don't try to awaken the cells of that child to an understanding, to more of a sensitivity of what's going on. Instead they just strike out, usually out of an embarrassment at not being in control of their child. Again, the child is taught to suppress his feelings, that they are not OK.

Right from the beginning, we teach each other to not be awake in the cells. Then we expect to grow up as adults and be fully alive! There's no way in the world this could happen. We end up with adults that are always cramming their emotions, and killing the spark of aliveness in their cells.

When the cells of the body are asleep, we're not hearing each other, much less ourselves. Many people become so anesthetized in their bodies, they end up being totally alone because nobody wants to be around them. These are people who are crippled by cellular repression. And yet, tremendous transformations have come about in people like this, through cellular awakening.

As immortals, we have to allow all of our emotions to come forth. We have to let go of our fears of getting out of control. We can no longer "put the lid" on each other or ourselves.

We don't lock into an image of the way it's got to happen. It is OK for adults to cry, to throw fits at times, even if that means laying on the floor and kicking our feet. We enjoy each other's expressions, no matter how they may come out. If there is some feeling we have with each other, negative or positive, we are able to express it to one another and hear each other.

☆ ☆ ☆ ☆ ☆

*I*t's funny in this world today, there is a lot of talk about becoming like a child. Yet, if somebody is acting like a child, we turn right around and tell them not to do it, to act like an adult. It can be very confusing.

The whole thing is, it's not a matter of acting like a child or an adult, it's acting out of the freedom of the cells of your body. Then, there is no age. There is

When you are acting out of the freedom of the cells of your body, there is no age.

no old or young. There's just a spontaneity in the cells of your body that we are not repressing anymore.

— James Russell

3

Eternal Life

M any people, when they first hear of physical immortality, assume that it has nothing to offer them, because they already have some form of eternal life through the spirit. But immortality goes far beyond anything offered by a life of the spirit. The eternity of the spirit world is no more than a pale promise compared to bodily immortality, no more than the earnest of our true inheritance.

Eternal life has taken many different forms. Christianity teaches us to believe in a life after death, in the forms of heaven and hell. The Eastern religions teach karmic law and reincarnation. Much New Age literature talks about past lives, and the schooling of the soul that takes place in a physical existence, in pursuit of some state of spiritual perfection. Even some naturalists tell us that death does not really exist, since the body returns to the earth when it dies, and from there feeds other life forms, in a continual renewal of life.

But once one comprehends physical immortality, all these beliefs become mere rationalizations, thin attempts to anesthetize man from the pain of death and separation, which is real.

Does it really make sense that spirit should return to physical form again and again just to become better spirit? If the physical world is truly base and inferior, then why does our soul have need of it? And, once we admit the possibility of immortality, does it not make more sense that we are here, time and again, to learn to stay here? Because this is where we are meant to be?

E ternal life, with its emphasis on the soul, has devalued the physical body, the unique identity of each physical form. The idea has been that, since the soul survives, nothing of value is lost when a person dies. The body is seen only as a source of limitation, something that gets in the way of a person's spiritual growth.

Nothing could be further from the truth. Each human form is uniquely and infinitely valuable. When any individual dies, the universe loses something that can never be replaced. Each one of us is an irreplaceable organ in a vast living body. All of us, even with our seeming imperfections, are invaluable.

Physical immortality stops the process of spiritual evolution, the cycle of life and death. Immortality allows us to get off the wheel of reincarnation. Karmic law comes to an end, in that we are no longer striving for a state of perfection. In this, we are no longer subject to paths, or sins. We are freed from the splits between heaven and hell, between life and death, between God and man. Immortality puts an end to the separation of spirit, soul and body.

We are ending the quest for a spiritual paradise in some other unknown dimension.

Physical immortality ends the concept of heaven or hell as a place of being after death. It offers instead the power of man to create his own heaven. We are ending the quest for a spiritual paradise in some other unknown dimension. We are taking the mystery out of heaven. In this, immortality is a fulfillment of the promise of Jesus, who according to the Bible said that heaven was within us. We are awakening to our power as divine creators.

P eople are sometimes reluctant to embrace physical immortality because they fear they will be losing something, in giving up the spiritual dimension. By committing fully to their bodies, they are afraid they will be forfeiting their spiritual side, their out of body experiences.

In reality, there is nothing to lose. There is no spiritual dimension separate from the physical body. Our separation of the two worlds is only a matter of perception, a reflection of the split that goes on in man's body.

> ### There is no spiritual dimension separate from the physical body.

Man's death-oriented consciousness tries to convince him there are two worlds, tempting him to be in the body part of the time, and in the spirit part of the time.

It is a trick. There has been a seduction there in that split, in the promise of keeping one foot in each world. In reality, as long as the consciousness remains split, the divided man is unstable, he's haunted by the separation between these two worlds, and never attains a feeling of wholeness.

In order to end this split, we must attain a total integration at a cellular level, which will bring about the end of aging and death within our own physical bodies. We must integrate with ourselves and with each other. This integration is necessary to let us see ourselves totally whole and complete as physical entities. It is only this integration that is capable of breaking through the illusions of death, to let us see ourselves as we really are.

One of the latest examples of man's split between the physical and spiritual is the practice of "channeling" entities from the spirit world. In these cases, ordinary people become mediums through which disembodied spirits are supposed to be speaking to us, conveying messages of great wisdom.

The great lie of channeling is that these messages are coming from some spirit separate from the speaker. Encoded in the cells of our bodies is the sum total of all people, men and women, that have ever lived. Everything that comes out of anyone's mouth is coming from the cells and atoms of their own body.

It is sad testimony to our lack of belief in each other, that we are more willing to give credence to a spirit speaking through a person, than we are to the person himself.

T he dream of eternal life has been a way of leaving the door open to giving up the bodies we have now, a way of hedging our bets on the physical world, in case our bodies disappoint us. In this, it has become another of man's excuses to reject the body, another way to convince us that our physical bodies aren't quite "it".

As immortals, though, we can accept no beliefs that separate or divide us from ourselves, or from one another, in any way.

> *We can accept no beliefs that separate or divide us from ourselves, or from one another, in any way.*

It takes all of our passion, every cell and atom of our bodies, to keep each other's lives, to have each other's bodies together on this planet. We cannot accept any concept of eternal life that would temper this passion, by offering us any easy escapes leading to death.

☆ ☆ ☆ ☆ ☆

*O*ne of the concepts has been that, if a body does die, then that person can come back in another form. The expression has been that the new form is really the same identity, that the person didn't really die, but just chose to take on a different body.

When I hear people talk like this, my body cries out, don't give me a replica, give me you! Your body is wonderful, why would you ever want to leave it? Why not just keep it and constantly move on and expand with it?

Your body is wonderful, why would you ever want to leave it?

It's never OK to lose any one of you. I love your form as it is now, and I will only continue to love it more. Not because you change your form, or transform to some other image or to a better body. I love your body the way it is now and the reality of it is, the longer I'm with you the more I come to love it the way it is now. I'm not trying to change your body so that I can love it, I'm getting to love your body more the way it is now.

That's the way it is, for me, and I don't want to be robbed. If I go out and buy a beautiful painting, a masterpiece, I want that masterpiece, I don't want a replica. That's the way it is with every human form. I don't want to get a replica, I want you.

— James Russell

☆ ☆ ☆ ☆ ☆

*O*nce there is the experiencing of that cellular integration, firstly with your own body, then with other immortal bodies around you, then there will be a synergistic energy that will be able to break through the death-oriented energy on the planet. As you are totally integrated, there will be that synergistic movement that will pierce that shield of death.

Then man will be able to see clearly his own body apart from this energy shield that keeps him blinded. It's like interference you see on television. It's a snowy picture that comes in. That's why he sees himself partly in the body and partly out of the body. It's all in perception.

— *Charles Paul*

✩ ✩ ✩ ✩ ✩

*W*hat we are about is the end of separation. Man has always separated spirit from body, made mind more important than the body, or body more important than the mind, whatever. What we're saying is that there is not one without the other. You don't cut your arm off because you might say it's not a part of your body, or because you think it's a lesser part.

The body is mind all over in

Spirit is part of the body.

every cell. You can't separate. When you're functioning out of the wholeness of that then you're getting the full capacity of the body, you're not limiting yourself.

Spirit is part of the body — I have yet to be able to experience an individual's spirit if his body wasn't here on the planet.

I know this idea is controversial, because a lot of people say they feel the energy of a person who has died. I feel that these people are just picking up the energy that is encoded in the cells of the body from when that individual was alive. If that person was never alive they wouldn't be able to have any feeling. If that person never existed on the planet, there would be no encoding in the cells of the body. When that person died, their body released an image of that life energy, but it is no longer alive, it's just an image of what once was alive. What people are picking up from these dead bodies is just the reflections of these images, being transmitted and reflected through space, then picked up like ghosts on a television.

— *James Russell*

☆ ☆ ☆ ☆ ☆

I n reality, there's no existence of another life without the flesh. These other dimensions do not really exist. It's the physical body that thinks about another life.

People aren't going to be physically immortal if they are creating all of these other forms of existence. They won't ever receive themselves as here to stay.

Once a person awakens to being physically immortal they don't want any other existence. They don't want a life after death because they are not dying. They don't want a spirit life, because they're enjoying them-

selves so much walking the face of the Earth.

For me, I don't have an afterlife, I don't need an afterlife because I'm here to stay. My energy doesn't go out in those directions.

— Bernadeane

☆ ☆ ☆ ☆ ☆

*I*t would be easier for you to believe my expression, for you to give it more credence, if I said God is telling me to tell you this. Or, this spirit, this ancient entity is communicating through me to tell you this. You would be astounded and amazed. You would listen. I could probably say anything to you and get away with it.

But, when I come in my own name and say, "Donald, I want to tell you this," it's a little tougher. Unless you knew I was 2,000 years old, or I was this spirit

> **"I don't have any need of spiritual entities, I look to you for my answers."**

that you would give credence to, it might be a little hard to believe me.

What we are about now is giving the credence to each other, looking at each other eye to eye, and saying: "I don't have any need of spiritual entities, I look to you for my answers. I have you. I believe in you."

— James Russell

4

Together Forever

Physical immortality is not a new concept. The yogis in the Himalayas and India focused on physical immortality for thousands of years. The ancient Chinese also were interested in physical immortality. But all these previous attempts failed, because they worked through isolation, and produced lone identities.

Mortal bodies on the planet are joined so intricately in a program of death, that they release a force that carries that program. They release an energy field on the planet that exerts a gravitational pull on the bodies who are awakening to being physically immortal.

This is why spiritual masters in times past often chose to isolate themselves in caves, to escape the energy vibration being released by death-oriented bodies. In doing so, though, they lost sight of their reason for living, and gave up their bodies.

Therefore, it takes an integration, a coming together, to live forever. From that integration, and responsiveness to our immortality, we do release, ourselves, an energy that is an antibody to the energy field of death.

This is one reason why it is imperative that those who are awakening on the planet, who are experiencing a cellular awakening, flow together to strengthen one another. Only by doing so can we release a new universal mind and intelligence that does not carry the program of death.

> *Only by flowing together can we release a new universal intelligence that does not carry the program of death.*

This is the intelligence that must now manifest on the planet from our immortal cellular body, through our being together.

This coming together is not always easy, or without challenges. But part of the beauty of sharing our lives with other immortals is that we do challenge each other, we stimulate each other to continually grow and expand. It's this sharing that brings out the best of all of us. Without it, we're not expressing everything that we are, and our immortality remains latent.

When we hear another immortal, what we might call the sound of our own voice, we react. We react to our own immortality being echoed from another, and there becomes a sharing. The more we share, the more we grow, the more we open up and expand together.

The coming together of our bodies produces an innate biological response. If we could see microscopically the responses and the exchange of the energy body, the energy patterns being emanated from the cells of our bodies when we are in the presence of one another, we could see a nurturing and nourishing taking place. There is an intercourse, an exchange of that energy with one another, and the cells are experiencing the benefit of that exchange. The result is a greater aliveness when we are in the presence of one another.

I mmortality not only requires us to come together, it requires us to stay together, forever. To keep each other's lives is to develop eternal immortal relationships. These must be immortal relationships in which we can never turn from, or on, one another.

It is only relationships like these that can make us feel safe and secure enough to open up everything that we are. This immortal commitment to each other frees us to experience a total passion for each other, a passion that keeps our very lives, a passion to keep each other on the planet, a passion that is stronger than death.

This is why we say that immortality is the deepest relationship that any of us have ever had and will have on this planet, the deepest sense of intimacy. It takes all that we are, being void of all the polarities and dualities in our bodies, being void of all death-oriented belief systems, to have that real cellular feeling with each other. It takes all that we are, 100% of us, to stir and keep each other's lives. So, immortality is the deepest intimacy any of us will have.

> *It takes all that we are, 100% of us, to stir and keep each other's lives.*

When we speak of immortal relationships, we are including many different kinds of relationships. We are certainly including intimate livings in which people sleep together. We are also including intimate livings in which people simply live together, without sharing a bed.

Beyond these, though, we are also talking about immortal communities, bringing people together who really want to live without death, who feel a passion for others on this planet. The Eternal Flame Foundation has created such a community, in Scottsdale, Arizona. This is not a commune, but an open community, that revolves around weekly meetings held by the Foundation.

As we move throughout the world, we find many who feel drawn to move here, to live with us in Scottsdale, and that is great. We welcome all immortals to join us. We will never discourage anyone from moving here.

Our primary intent is not to pull people to Scottsdale, however. Not everyone will be able to move to Scottsdale, or will want to. Our goal is to create what we are throughout the world. We want to establish intimate immortal communities all around the globe, so that bodies awakening to their immortality can gravitate to these centers. We want to cover the earth with a network of immortal communities, all in cellular contact with one another. Our vision is to create a global cellular body.

☆ ☆ ☆ ☆ ☆

When you have that feeling, beyond a concept or a philosophy, when you have that total realization that you're with somebody forever and they're with you, that you don't have to fear that division from each other anymore, you don't have to fear that you're going to impart war on one another, and you know there is no reason or way you can leave or forsake each other, then it brings out a whole new level of safety that has never been experienced before.

It's this feeling that allows us to truly "take the lid off," which means opening up every facet of our personalities and our feelings with each other, without fear of being left or rejected. We have opened up a whole new freedom for each other because the biggest fear that most people have in opening themselves up is that they are going to be rejected if they do so, that it's not acceptable.

This is the freedom of expression and the flow of the cells of our bodies that have never felt free to flow.

This fear of rejection has not only kept the individual from being a true individual, it's also suppressed the flow between the bodies that have been together, the flow between the immortal cells that really spark and stir each other, that unleash the immortality of our flesh.

I feel the very core of what keeps us alive is contained within our bodies, but our coming together is what unleashes that power.

I feel the very core of what keeps us alive is contained within our bodies, but our coming together is what unleashes that power. You could call it the anointing, the biological responses that are there that flow with each other throughout the body and heal scars that go deep and have been there for thousands of years, from wars and conflicts and divisions that have gone on since man has existed.

— James Russell

5

God and
Immortality

Most of humanity has always believed in some form of divinity, or that which has been called a "higher power". The greatest percentage of humanity has always had a sense of spirituality, of limitlessness, of eternity, some vibrations they were not fully aware of, which they could not fully comprehend.

And yet, something has always prevented man from claiming that divinity as his own. This has been his death programming, his acceptance of the inevitability of death. As long as he believed that his physical body must die, he had to place all of his divinity in some other realm, which was supposedly not subject to death.

Because death was inevitable, humankind created all of that which is represented to be the invisible. Man attached his higher self to an invisible God in another dimension. He then aspired to that dimension, but always had the feeling that he had to get out of the body, had to leave the gravity of his physical form, in order to attain that place. At the same time, he began to believe that God, in this other dimension, was the source of his aliveness, and that his physical form was dependent for its energy on this external source.

All of this has created a mystique of the invisible, the ethereal, the cosmic dimensions which exist apart from the physical body. This has become a mythology of the unseen. And it is this mythology which has created a tremendous split in man, the split between the physical and the spiritual, the temporal and the eternal, between our devils and our gods.

This need to externalize God, and all of the resulting splits in man, have been caused by his death programming, by the thoughts fed into him from the time of his birth, from an ancestry that accepted death as inevitable.

The truth is our bodies are beautifully and wonderfully designed and without limitation. There is no difference between our physical bodies and that which man has perceived to be invisible.

This is not a denial of spirit. We are spiritual beings. We are physical beings. But the spirit is not something apart from the body. It all takes place right here in us.

We have energy bodies which are the product of the chemical actions and reactions taking place within the cells of our bodies, not the cause of that action. It is a mistake to think of our bodies as inert matter that is animated only through the injection of some spiritual energy whose source is God. The source of this energy, this spirit, is the nuclei of the very cells in our bodies, the chemical action that takes place there. This energy is very tangible, it is what allows us to feel the spirit, or feel the thoughts, of another person.

The source of what we call spirit is in the nuclei of the very cells of our bodies.

Science has demonstrated that each cell carries the full image of the total human form. This is why the life energy emitted from our cells projects what we call an energy body, or spirit body. It is the experience of this spirit body which people often identify with altered states, and are sometimes called "out of body" experiences. Yet, the source of this spirit body is the physical body itself.

There is a process called Kirlian photography which has allowed us to capture images of energy bodies leaving their physical bodies. This is the energy being released from the cells as they die. The image of the form is released to the atmosphere but it has no manifestation. Its origin is here, and it is a manifestation of the physical even in the "invisible" world. Without the body, there is no life. There is no life to the spirit. It takes the generation of the body itself being alive to give power. We are the nucleus for all power, not some source outside of us.

U p until now, man has always had to move in the name of God, he has not been able to claim that power for himself. That's why so many false Christs have come forth, because they want to come in the name of a previous avatar or Christ.

But we come in our names, we sign our own names to what we are saying. It's very powerful. Everything that man has attributed to God or the spirit world has always come forth from the body of man. And yet, immortals have

> *We do not come to you in the name of God, we come in our own names.*

much to be thankful for in God. In our death-oriented society it has often been God that has kept our dreams of immortality alive. God has represented for us all that is good and wonderful, omnipotent, omniscient and omnipresent, all that is without limitation. As a result, God has been, for many of us, a conscience of paradise lost, a stepping stone to immortality.

Some people may feel a lot of conflict in the

way we dismiss God. To those people, we want to say, if there is a God then there is no one doing his will better. If there is a God, then he isn't seeking our acknowledgment, he doesn't want us setting him up as an idol. What he wants is the living abundantly of one another. That's why we feel, if he does exist, we're serving him better than anyone has ever served him on the planet.

A nother source of man's belief in God has been his search for a source of death and destruction in the world. Man has felt a need to identify a cause for natural disasters, and so has called them "acts of God".

It is a mistake, however, to confuse a destructive power with a higher power. Nuclear warfare, with its ability to destroy absolutely, is not a higher power. Because one nation has the power to destroy another does not mean it is a greater nation. Just because there is a power that man fears does not mean that it is a higher power.

This identification of God as a destroyer has been used by man as a justification for his own destructive urges. God has been, in a sense, an alter ego, a being on which we could project all of our judgments and aggressive urges, rather than taking responsibility for them ourselves. We've created an idol outside of ourselves to give us credence to attack and destroy each other. This has become yet another tool to suppress our aliveness.

Man has also concluded that God must exist through his search for his own beginnings. God has been man's answer to the question, "Who created the universe?" But researchers still cannot find the beginning of the universe, no matter how many millions of years they go back.

Just as the universe has no beginning, so is man without beginning. Man has always been. This is a hard thing for most people to accept because they image man in just one way, with two arms, two legs, as he exists today. At one time, though, man may have been in a totally different form, even consisting of only one cell. But that cell was still a body.

Just as man may trace his lineage back to a single-celled organism, it does not stop here, with our current forms. Putting an end to death does not mean putting an end to evolution. Evolution has resulted from a spontaneous

> *We are expanding so rapidly that we no longer need death as a means of growth.*

generation which has been our way of expanding or growing as a species.

We have now evolved to the point where death is no longer necessary, but this does not mean that change and growth will stop. Evolution has been a means for our species to change and adapt and this expansion is still essential. Being immortal does not mean an end to change, it means an acceleration of change. We are growing and expanding so rapidly that we no longer need death as a means of growth, physically or spiritually, as individuals or as a species.

A re we all that there is then? Is there no greater power outside of ourselves? In a sense, there is. In the Bible, Jesus instructed the people "Love the Lord, your God, with all your heart, with all your might, with all your soul." But, the next verse says that this commandment is fulfilled in that, "You love your neighbor as yourself." He was seeking, even in that statement, to end the mystery of God.

There is one power greater than any one individual, and that is two of us together. And there is yet a greater power than two, which is three of us together. So you can say that God is the sum total of all that we are together. This is the truest sense in which God can be said to exist. This is the sense in which we, ourselves, awaken to being the living God.

☆ ☆ ☆ ☆ ☆

A *school bus goes down the street, crashes, all the kids burn and we say, "Oh, it must have been God's will." That wasn't God's will, that was a result of our death programming, our belief in the inevitability of death. That accident was created by a death consciousness. God's will is that we thrive and live and love and support each other to live immortally.*

— James Russell

☆ ☆ ☆ ☆ ☆

I would like to think, if I was just one cell at one time in the past, that I took the form I am today out of a joy of wanting to express myself better. I can express myself better as the living form I am with vocal cords, two arms, two legs, two eyes to see you and so forth. Whereas at one time, as a cell, I could express myself but it was limited. But out of the joy of my expression, I evolved. I transformed myself through spontaneous generation out of that joy and my desire to express. Now, as the species I am today, my ability to express my joy and feelings and passion is much greater.

— James Russell

☆ ☆ ☆ ☆ ☆

God has taken on many forms in my expansion. When I was a child growing up, God was my creator and he was the creator of the Universe to me. He was everything great and wonderful and I loved Him with all of my heart. I gave to Him totally. He was my friend, that which was closer than a brother. He was there for me always because I didn't know what it was to be intimate with my family, friends, or people with whom I would come in contact. I didn't know what that was like. God was my intimate relationship.

But, as I began to wake up, God started taking on different forms to me. It was then I began to find God within. It was wonderful. As I went along, I became God.

Then physical immortality kept taking on different forms for me. It became different than when I initially awakened. It's not just an experience anymore. To me, today, physical immortality is me walking the face of the Earth.

God is the same way. As I have changed and moved and become more alive, more alive with you, I find no need of God. I can only speak from my own personal experience in all of this, because that's what is real for me. It was then that you became my God.

You are not my God. You are my life. You are my everything.

Now, though, I don't experience this to be my reality any longer. It isn't that I have done away with God. I haven't given up God, but I have changed. Therefore, I don't experience the necessity of God as I once did, because I found you.

You are not my God. You are my life. You are my living. You are my everything. You are not my God as I am not God to you, I'm Bernadeane to you. I'm all that I am to you. I am all that you see and allow me to be.

I say to people, I am not here to take away your God. But, for me, you took the place of my God.

— Bernadeane

6

Immortal Passion

Immortal passion is a feeling for each other which is stronger than death. This is what it takes to experience immortality: a feeling of living for ourselves and for one another. This passion itself is stronger than death.

Many people attempt to struggle with death. They try to make themselves so strong physically that death cannot touch them. Some try to protect themselves by building an empire around nutrition. Others try to overpower death through an intellectual struggle, by flexing their muscle of knowledge. Yet others grapple with death through their religious beliefs and practices. All of these attempts fail, because they make the mistake of trying to beat death on its own territory, by using death's own tools of ego and domination.

It's not by struggle that we will conquer death, but by our feeling for ourselves and one another. This is the feeling we call the "anointed energy". It is the infinite, all-forgiving, unconditional love we have always seen to be an attribute of God. Up until now, we've never believed ourselves capable of this kind of love, much less the capacity to live on this planet forever.

We are finding we are capable of that kind of love, we are surprising each other by how deeply we

> *It's not by struggle that we will conquer death, but by our feeling for ourselves and one another.*

can feel. It goes on and on, it is an unlimited love. It's a love so strong that not even death, should it try, can touch it.

Down through the ages, the religious ideal has typically been for man to attain a quiet, meditative state of being. This is the belief which is predominant on the planet today, that quiet contemplation is the most effective way to get in touch with yourself, especially with your "spiritual" self. But we are finding that this is not necessarily the case. Quiet meditation is a wonderful state, but it is not our only goal, it is not a "higher" state. As immortals, our goal is to feel and express our full aliveness, whatever form we may take.

The intensity of immortal passion can sometimes feel unsettling to bodies that are not prepared for it. People sometimes react to our energy by saying that we are too emotional, too zealous, or too loud. We are finding as immortals we can never be too much for each other. On the contrary, the very intensity of our passion for one another is what keeps our lives.

The release of immortal energy can also be very healing. Illnesses are sometimes nothing but blocked energy where toxins are stored. In the full expression of our aliveness there can be a release of that energy, and of the toxins, and people can actually be healed.

There can be no immortal passion without a commitment to stay with each other. This commitment is necessary to foster a complete flowing of everything we are feeling with each other. If we are afraid of leaving each other, we will not be willing to open ourselves up totally. But an immortal passion also fosters this commitment. When we are feeling this passion, we do not want to leave each other ever.

To act completely from an immortal passion brings about a wonderful feeling; we sometimes call it a feeling of being anointed. It is such a feeling of freedom, of aliveness, to be free of the survival consciousness that has guided our actions for most of our lives, and to be motivated purely from a passion for immortal living.

The term "anointing" has a rich significance for us. Literally, to anoint means to rub with oil, especially for the purpose of consecration. It implies a physical touch, a laying on of hands. It also gives a sense of penetration, as the oil penetrates the skin. The idea of consecrating one another is also very important.

This anointed passion that we are speaking of is not something new. It is something that springs from the depths of man's body, something which has always been there, but man has attributed it to some source outside himself. It's the same feeling that is generated from a chant or mantra. It is what the Pentecosts have experienced in

> *This is the immortal passion that is stronger than death itself.*

receiving the baptism of the holy spirit, in speaking in tongues. It is what Leonard Orr and others talk about in the feeling of being rebirthed. It is a response from within the body itself of waking up, of coming alive. This is the immortal passion that is stronger than death itself.

☆ ☆ ☆ ☆ ☆

W e're not going to beat death by might or by strength. In fact, we are never going to beat death at all.

It's not for us to fight death. The intelligence of death is well established, well encoded in this world. We will not change it by might or by power.

The only way we will experience immortality is by unleashing that which we are, that anointed energy, that immortal substance innate in the cells of our bodies. We will not achieve immortality by analyzing how we are going to do it, by trying to figure it out or by looking for a formula. It will only happen through the unleashed flesh and bone bodies of one another.

We won't be immortal by trying to beat against the wall of death, by trying to tear it down. We must outlive it, we must plunge through it. It means we just make a hole the size of a pinhead, and say, "Hey, let's not worry about the wall, let's plunge through that pinhole."

— *James Russell*

☆ ☆ ☆ ☆ ☆

W hen you feel total aliveness, you are not seeking to impose any structure on your expression, and your expression is not being controlled by an external consciousness. You are being motivated by an implosion that is taking place on a cellular level within your body. You cannot confine this passion, you must have free reign to really move, totally unchartered and uncontrolled. This is the energy felt by immortal bodies.

— *Charles Paul*

J esus had to be very passionate, animated, and alive to even dare to go into the temple and begin to turn the money changers' tables upside down. There was an anger that was in his voice. When he would speak to others who were resisting what he was trying to bring forth, sometimes he wasn't a lamb at all, he was a lion.

— *Charles Paul*

☆ ☆ ☆ ☆ ☆

I mmortal passion involves a commitment to one another. It means being together forever, maybe not in the same locality, but it does mean being together forever.

We're bringing about a world today where separation is going to be unheard of. It's not even going to be remembered. Immortal bodies will not even know what separation is all about. It is something that was passed on to us by way of an ancestry who were oriented unto death; death means separation.

Already, in our world there is no death. Immortal passion automatically brings about a commitment unto one another where there is no death or separation, no divorcing one another.

Charles was reading to me an article out of the newspaper that was about a couple who live in Russia and they were celebrating their 103rd wedding anniversary. The woman is 118 and the man is 122. In their part of Russia, divorce is unheard of.

That story said a lot to me. There's something about not experiencing separation that brings about longevity *and long life. There is something about immortal passion that brings about eternity, "foreverness", a being together forever.*

— Bernadeane

☆ ☆ ☆ ☆ ☆

*M*oving from an anointing is moving from an immortal passion. Rather than feeling a survival consciousness of trying to break through something, you're already there putting balm on one another. It's like you are putting an ointment on one another's bodies.

It is when we are moving from an anointing that we are really life to each other, are really lifting each other. It's like an oil that goes through every cell and atom of our bodies.

This is something very real that we are talking about.

It's like an oil that goes through every cell of our bodies.

People have told us they actually experienced the feeling of something going through their bodies when we have expressed; we've had that same sensation with each other. It's nothing mystical. We are all very aware when we're acting out of survival and when we're feeling the anointing. It's an identification with our bodies, instead of a survival consciousness that we thought was us.

That's when we're really alive, when we anoint one another with oil, our passion.

— James Russell

7

The Cellular Connection

T he bond between immortals is something special, something which goes beyond the normal ties of family and friends. It is a deep cellular connection, one which cannot abide any form of separation, including the separation of death.

We have already talked about the cellular awakening which takes place when one truly responds to immortality. The next step beyond awakening is the immortal connection with other bodies. This cellular connection is absolutely vital—without it, one has only made a connection with another truth or philosophy.

When we say that the connection is cellular, we mean that it goes beyond the usual limitations of the mind. It is not a connection based on our images or thoughts of one other. Instead, it is based on a cellular hunger for each other which is felt all over, in every cell of our bodies.

People wonder what they have to do to become immortal. Immortality is not the result of a thought process, nor does it result directly from any behavior or practices which you adopt. Some have tried, for example, to achieve immortality by becoming vegetarians, by fasting, or through meditation. All of these practices can be complimentary to an immortal life, but you can't achieve

> *A cellular connection is a direct contact between the cells of our bodies.*

immortality solely through these practices, or any others. In fact, such practices can be draining instead of nurturing, if they are performed as a labor, just as a means to an end.

A cellular connection is a direct contact between the cells of our bodies which bypasses the brain and all of the mental processes. That's why sometimes individuals who initially opposed us with their minds have come back later. Often, the first reaction is from a mentality which has been programmed with some rigid belief structure.

People have come back to us later, though, and expressed they were now hearing what we had first said to them. A seed had been planted at the original meeting, not in their minds, but in their bodies. The cells of their bodies were awakened at that moment, and a deathless intelligence was released to overpower the intellectual program of death within the body. This is the power of the cellular connection.

There is a language of the body which is biological, which is a world apart from the mortal existence we have come to accept as normal. There is a network of communication which is going on that is totally separate and apart from our conscious awareness. Unless we tap into this, through whatever means, we will never experience immortality. This is what we mean when we say that the connection must be cellular.

This book is an invitation for you to awaken to your own physical immortality. That is not enough, however. We want to be cellularly connected to you, and you to us. What we are talking about is not a vague, spiritual concept—it is personal and physical. We want to make physical contact with you, to experience the uniqueness of you. And we want you to have an opportunity to make a cellular connection with us. You and we, and the connection we have, are more important than anything you will read in this book.

W hen you are cellularly connected to someone, you will find you cannot do without them in your life. Without those to whom you are cellularly connected, there is no living in an immortal life. There would be death for us without one another. This is the feeling of having a cellular connection. This is what causes us to experience such a great joy and nourishment—this cellular connection. Biologically we need each other and keep each other.

This is not to say that you have to see someone every day, or every week, to maintain this connection. You can be at opposite ends of the earth, and go for long periods without physical contact, and still be connected. What's important is you both feel the attraction in your bodies, and experience a physical certainty that you will be part of each other's lives forever.

And yet, at the same time, physical separation can be used to try to break, or deny the cellular connection. Many people have deep fears of intimacy and commitment and all of these fears can be surfaced and brought forward by contact with an immortal body. A person who fears intimacy may respond by leaving, giving you assurances they are one with you, wherever they are, and therefore, there is no true separation. In this sense, the claim of a cellular connection may be used as an excuse for what is really an avoidance of intimacy.

All immortal relationships should be based on a cellular connection but this does not mean they should all be the same or should be equal. Every immortal relationship, like every immortal person, is unique and individual. The common denominator is the cellular connection, but different relationships will have varying levels, and various kinds, of intimacy.

Immortals have a rich variety of relationships: from intimate daily livings to long-distance friendships. An intimate living will be with those you can't stand to be away from, even for a day, but you will not need everyone to be included in your daily living. And yet, no matter what the relationship, or the frequency of contact, there will be the ongoing need for each other. This is the cellular connection.

Some people are afraid of admitting they need another. They think a need means they lack something in themselves. This is not so. A need for another person is a wonderful quality, an immortal quality.

Some people are afraid to admit they need another.

A need for material things may indicate a lack but needing another person is a true expression of being physically immortal.

A cellular connection is the deepest passion two bodies can feel for each other. This is why people sometimes confuse it with sex. For many, sexual passion has been the only means of escaping their minds and really feeling their bodies. It has also been, up until now, the greatest way mankind has known to share all the depths of our feelings with each other, to really open ourselves up to each other. As a result, many people, when they first feel a cellular connection, associate it with sex, and even feel that it is not complete until it has been fulfilled in a sexual manner.

But, there is a cellular connection which exceeds what we've ever known. People equate it to sex because that is all they have had to compare it to. In reality it goes far beyond sex, and is complete in and of itself.

H aving a cellular connection with someone does not mean that everything will be smooth sailing between you from that point on. Far from it! Everything you can imagine may come up in your relationship. You may feel a profound love for a person one day, and the next day that same person may seem to have the most hated characteristics you could possibly imagine.

But a cellular connection goes beyond love and hate. When the connection is made, it makes no difference what you experience with each other, you find nothing can shake your foundation with each other in the cells of your body.

As an immortal, you'll experience with a person all of the things you hate about them. You'll also experience all of the things you love. But, in it all, your connection with them won't be based on your love or your hate. Instead, it will be based on an unshakeable passion for each other, a connection that goes far beyond any love that has ever been felt. It will be based on a

A cellular connection goes beyond love.

cellular knowing that you are with each other forever. This is the passion which is stronger than death.

It is for this reason that the cellular connection offers us our only hope of achieving humanity's dreams of world peace and harmony. How else can we come together on this planet, with all of our different beliefs, different ways, and different personalities? It's not possible without a cellular connection.

This is what we are so desirous to spread throughout the planet — the immortal, biological connection, and the intelligence that a seed is after its own kind, and we are the immortal seed. What we want is nothing less than a global cellular body.

☆ ☆ ☆ ☆ ☆

W e are bypassing the mind that would accept immortality. We are bypassing the mind of truth that says death is inevitable. We are bypassing the programmed mind that is in alignment with the acceptance of death from its ancestry that has been in operation for generation upon generation.

We are bypassing the mind that would accept immortality. We're going right to the core.

We're going right to the core. We're going right to the seed life biologically to awaken that life to begin to respond. We're seeing it happening.

— Charles Paul

☆ ☆ ☆ ☆ ☆

T here's a fine line here because, when you have a cellular connection, there are no biological boundaries between each other anymore. So, no matter where you are on the planet, there are no boundaries between you.

But then you have the person who is still running from intimacy, running from that connection, who will use "oneness of each other" to still get away and not fuse totally.

— James Russell

8

The Genetics of Death

People experiencing any sort of personal expansion frequently report other people in their life often resist the growth they are feeling. Many times, the people closest to you seem to have the most invested in your staying the same. They may have even chosen you, often unconsciously, specifically because of some limitation of yours that you are now ready to leave behind. They may feel comfortable with you just the way you are and your growth may make them feel threatened.

Unfortunately, family members often fall into this category. In addition to the possibility of their having chosen you for some limitation, they may even have had a hand in raising you, and creating that limitation in you. Additionally, family members usually feel a great investment in you, and feel they have more to lose if you change in any way which threatens them, or their relationship with you.

Physical immortality is the greatest expansion you can ever experience. It is also the commitment to continue expanding, to continue growing, to grow beyond all your limitations, including that of death. Therefore, it is not surprising if others around you, including members of your family, feel threatened when you begin to awaken from the sleep of death.

Physical immortality often poses a special threat to the family structure. One of the enticements of the family structure has been the belief you can never find a greater love outside of the family. No one will ever love you more than your mother, for example. The family has also been portrayed as more permanent than other parts of your life. They say "Others may come and go, but your family will never leave you," or "Blood is thicker than water." Such is the gravitational pull that has kept the family together.

As one begins to waken to immortality, however, one begins to feel a pull to others who have awakened. And, as new immortal relationships are formed, one finds a deeper, more satisfying and more sustaining love than that offered by any mortal relationship, even with family members. What's more, one finds more permanent love, love that does not just continue "until death do us part." And so, the family ties begin to loosen, family members who are not joining in your awakening begin to feel this unraveling and feel threatened.

Other family members can often sense something happening even without your speaking of it. In awakening to being physically immortal, a cellular awakening shakes the family tree. Because it is a biological awakening, immediately there are different signals that begin to be transmitted. There is a different intelligence from which one begins to operate. There is a different energy pattern that one begins to emanate. The family tree can become very threatened by all this, even without any conscious awareness as to what is going on.

Once you begin to express to others about your awakening, the resistance can be even stronger. People often have a deep investment in death. Undoubtedly they have had loved ones die, and have consoled themselves with the belief they will meet again in heaven. They may have purchased life insurance policies, or a family plot at the cemetery.

> *People often have a deep investment in death.*

As a result, they may feel profoundly threatened by the possibility of physical immortality.

At times, someone's investment in death can even be so intense they would actually wish to see you die, because that would prove them right! People find this hard to believe, but it can sometimes be true. Even if they don't actually wish you to die outright, they may feel relieved if you become ill, or show signs of aging. They may secretly, or openly, desire this.

We want to make it clear that we are not indicting families in general. We have experienced immortal families that are great support systems for their members. These are families that are held together by real feelings of love, that allow intimacy, that encourage their members to continually grow and expand, and that are open to new ideas, new experiences and new people. This sort of family is wonderful and nourishing.

Unfortunately, many families are not like this. Many are dominated by a family structure that would seek to confine its members to their ancestral roles. Many families attempt to perpetuate genetic patterns that are unto our death. They often impose a rigidity on their members: fixed patterns of thinking, of feeling, of living, and of dying. Many practice a subtle form of discrimination against "outsiders," by insisting that "blood is thicker than water." Often they try to define their members solely by the roles they fill: mother, father, son, daughter. In doing so, they too often make the family more important than the person—after all, in the mortal world, it has been the family that has survived, outliving all of its individual members.

What we want to emphasize is that you end any allegiance to death in your own body. We do not recommend that you run from your family. People sometimes feel so much resistance from their families they feel the only answer is to not be around them. We do not advocate this sort of reaction. No one is to be alienated on this planet. As immortals, we cannot turn away from anyone, we cannot treat them as if they were bad people. We must give them all of ourselves, give them our total passion. They will make their choice of what they want to do with our passion. We cannot make that choice for them.

At the same time, we must resist any senti-mental feelings that would bind us to our family. We must give them our pas-sion, but this passion cannot be based on any feelings of senti-

We must give a passion that is free from any feelings of sentimentality.

mentality. What we have seen, so often, is these sentimental and sympathetic feelings ensnare people and pull them back into their genetic pat-terns of death. We cannot give credence to death in any form, no matter how strongly we may be tempted at times by a sentimental allegiance to family. We must always make a clear sound, a clear distinction, between that which is unto death and that which is physically immortal.

Keep in mind, too, that one can run from their family and still have their genetics operating right inside them all of the time. As they say, "You can take a person out of the hills, but you can't take the hills out of the person." Genetic patterns run deep, and are not easily uprooted. Don't make the mistake of thinking you can break your genetic ties simply by avoiding your family.

We are not of death. And yet we have been programmed to die. We must be constantly sensitive to that which is truly us and that which is our imposed programming. It is so subtle. The ancestral programming of death can be like a thin veil, hiding the light. Once it is removed, there you are, the brightness of you! We see at times people remove the veil only to put it back on. They will be experiencing the brightness of their light, then they will draw the veil back to wear almost like a mask. The veil comes from the consciousness of the old, and it's not really you anymore.

☆ ☆ ☆ ☆ ☆

*E*ven though we don't alienate ourselves from anyone—including the family that gave birth to us— because of what we are experiencing in who we are, we also don't find a communion with them. We're not to feel badly about this. There is something that happens when one awakens to being physically immortal. In a sense, you don't have anything in common. There is no place to really meet one another. There just isn't a communion together.

I think a lot of people have a problem with this. Once they awaken they have a problem with how to communicate with family, because there is a change that does take place and you don't want to be rude to them. The whole answer is for you to be who you really are when you're with your family, to not stick yourself in the *closet when you're with them, to let them know who you really are. Then it's clean, and there can be a friendship there. But it won't be the depths of what you have with one who meets you in all that you are.*

— Bernadeane

☆ ☆ ☆ ☆ ☆

I *was expressing to an aunt of mine about a stomach disorder I no longer desired to keep. I was expressing that I was absolutely going to end the problem, by my resistance and refusal to claim it any longer.*

I suddenly felt a vibration of rage coming from her and I asked her what was going on. She burst out crying and said, "I want you to be **It is not necessarily our genes that transmit these illnesses to us.** *proud you have inherited the stomach condition from your grandfather!"*

She actually wanted me to feel pride in the fact I'd inherited the stomach condition from her father. I just looked at her and said, "I'm free from that genetic." She became extremely emotional. From this experience I could see the entire picture of how the process works to keep aging and disease alive in the family structure.

There is an unspoken bond in many of these diseases. We often feel there is nothing we can do about our genetics. We can be made to feel we have to make the best of whatever genetic tendencies we have inherited from our family. But we are seeing that this no longer has to be our reality. It is not necessarily our genes that transmit these weaknesses and illnesses to us — it is our pride in our genetics, our hanging on to them. All we have to do to be free of them is to let them go.

— Charles Paul

☆ ☆ ☆ ☆ ☆

*D*eath was presented to us by way of our ancestry. It was placed upon us. We would have never chosen it. This is why we're having to look at it just as it is. It's not that we're against our ancestry and the people they are, we're just aware of what actually transpires. We are literally clipping the ties that bind us to that which causes death.*

They, without a doubt most of them anyway, were innocent in a sense. But, once a person becomes consciously aware, whether or not they're cellularly aware, they aren't innocent anymore. There is a tremendous responsibility which rests upon the person who becomes even consciously aware that death is not necessary.

Really, for us now, death is impossible. Now that we've clipped that tie, that bond to an ancestral inheritance of death, we are absolutely free. It's not possible for us to go that way.

Now, when we give birth to people, we are not passing onto them the death. We're passing to them that which we are, which is immortality. That is their inheritance.

— Bernadeane

*T*here is a new genetic family that is appearing on the planet right now. We are now going to produce our own kind in which the memory of a family structure that dies is going to be wiped away, and death and hell shall be cast into the lake of fire in our coming.

The former things won't even come into mind. I want the former things in our own bodies, the memory molecules, the memory patterns that have been in our own bodies, to be wiped away, to not even be remembered. We won't remember that we ever belonged to a family of death — we will know that we have always belonged to the family of immortals.

I know, even now, when I become sluggish in my body, when I become foggy, I am finding that it has to do with a genetic of a memory molecule which is seeking to work within my flesh. I'm really beginning to sense this.

We are absolutely to give no space for the memory of an intelligence that can confuse us and cause us to become sluggish and sleep the sleep which has been of our fathers, according to our biological ancestry. Now, our biological ancestry is the family of immortals. I like that — "the family of immortals!"

We are the family of immortals — we have always been.

We are the family of immortals — we have always been. Everyone of us has always felt that we belonged somehow. Now we're finding our own.

— *Charles Paul*

9

Immortal Emotions

P art of the duality that has led to man's death has been his denial of his emotions. In the mortal world, emotions have been labeled as negative. Whereas rational thought has been considered a product of the mind, and the "finer feelings" have been attributed to the soul or spirit, emotions have been seen as coming from the body, and therefore have been considered suspect. In order to end this duality, and reclaim their bodies, immortals must acknowledge and express all of their emotions.

Our culture does much to discredit our emotions and the honest expression of them. There is a whole etiquette governing the proper display of emotions. Some times are considered better than others for showing emotions.

If someone calls you "emotional," it usually

implies that you are undependable and even somewhat foolish. If you freely express your emotions, you may be called too loud, too intense, a zealot. In general, emotions are seen as signs of weakness to be covered up.

From the spiritual, metaphysical and rational worlds, we have been advised to put "mind over matter." The mind is given preeminence

Why do we fear our emotions so much?

and is identified as an entity apart from the body. As a result, we have been told that emotions must be kept in check, they must be controlled, because they are considered to be a baser sense of feeling. They have been identified with the physical body, as being of a baser substance, and of operating on a lower dimension, or a lower vibratory level.

On a more practical level, books and magazine articles have been written about how to get ahead by controlling and manipulating your emotions and those of others. The general advice is to hide your emotions so that no one knows what you're really feeling. If you are disturbed, or hurt, or angry about something, then keep it a secret, because these emotions are considered signs of weakness. These writings teach you how to put on the appearance of being fine when you really aren't.

This emotional suppression has been imposed especially on the males of our society. For example, it is acceptable for women to cry but not for men. If a father spanks his son and as a result his son doesn't cry anymore, then his father may tell him that he is a little man now. This is considered part of a boy's training, to learn how to hide his tears. It is supposed to be a sign of strength, and yet it is this so-called "strength" that causes men in our society to die so much earlier than women, on the whole.

Why do we fear our emotions so much? Our survival consciousness, our belief that we live in a "dog-eat-dog" world, has caused us to distrust sharing our emotions with each other, for fear they will be used against us.

We have also learned to distrust others' emotions because they are so often used for manipulation. We see people being depressed, or sick, or suffering from some tragedy, and using their condition to control someone else by evoking sympathy or guilt.

So we have been taught to fear our emotions because they are so powerful, and because we have generally used them against each other.

All of this negative programming has often caused us to stifle our real feelings and in turn stifle the cellular awakening of physical immortality.

T he truth is that it's not a weakness to let somebody see your real feelings, to let them know that they've hurt you or they've made you angry. That's honesty, and that's the only way we're going to be able to give each other a real feeling about what's happening in our bodies together.

So often, we stifle and suppress our emotions from fear of hurting each other. I am afraid that I will hurt you by telling you how I really feel, or I am afraid that you will lash out at me, if I tell you a feeling of mine that you don't want to hear. We see each other so often only as potential sources of pain for each other. As a result, we spend all of our energy trying to protect ourselves from each other.

To be immortal, we must see things differently. First, we must realize that we will never leave each other, even through death. Our ultimate fear has always been abandonment.

> *We must see each other as sources of love, joy and nourishment.*

Once we remove that prospect and realize that we will stay with each other through anything and everything, we find that any other pain we might sometimes cause each other is insignificant in comparison.

Second, we must see each other as sources of love, joy, and nourishment. We are not that to each other that will take our lives, but that which will keep our lives forever. The expression of our true, deep feelings for each other nourishes us in a way that nothing else can. In this light, honest emotional expression is always welcome, because it always leads to these deep feelings, no matter what it may seem like at the time.

As physical immortals we are creating an environment in which it is safe to show our emotions, to let others know that we are hurt or angry. We are able to express anger, joy, fear and all emotions without having them turned against us. At the same time, we are creating the ability to experience others' emotions without fear of being manipulated by them. We must be able to share true, honest emotions with each other and use them to nourish one another, rather than using them against each other. In this movement, there is a healthiness to be experienced in our emotions that has never been felt before.

In such an immortal environment we are able to get to the bottom of our emotions, and often find them to be very deep feelings, rather than the emotional whims we are used to. The feelings that are revealed then help bring about a deep, physical connection with each other.

N one of this is to say that all emotional expressions are healthy. A person can be so totally enveloped in an emotion that he becomes buried in it. One can get buried in grief, for example, or emotions surrounding some negative drama going on. But in these cases it is not the emotions that are unhealthy, or even the expression of those emotions, but the inability to let go of them, and move beyond them. One can become addicted to certain emotions, like anything else, and addictions are never healthy.

Ultimately, having and expressing emotions is part of being alive, and can only lead to further aliveness. As immortals, we rejoice in our emotions, as we do in our physical bodies.

I f you hide your emotions from someone, then you are only giving them a part of yourself. For example, let's suppose you always tell everyone you feel good all of the time. Whenever anybody asks you how you are feeling, you just say, "Oh, I feel great!"

But maybe at times you are not feeling so great, and you do have something that's bothering you, but you don't want to show that to anyone. Then you're only giving a small part of yourself. You're being superficial and not letting other people know where you really are. You are robbing yourself of a nourishment you could receive, and you are robbing others who are around you as well.

— James Russell

*A*s immortals, we must develop a deep sense of vulnerability with each other. We do not have to protect ourselves. We don't have to defend ourselves. We can be real with each other every moment. We can let down our guards and show all of our feelings.

In doing this, we make our feelings and emotions something healthy. We deepen the sense of communication with each other. We give each other that stability so that we can then, absolutely, have a communication with each other that is very, very deep.

— *James Russell*

☆ ☆ ☆ ☆ ☆

I can't see the significance of an immortal body walking around without any emotions. It just seems like feelings and emotions are all part of being physically immortal. It all goes together.

It takes the emotions to cause an immortal person to unfold, to develop as an immortal body. It takes the emotions to stir us, whatever kind of emotions they are. It matters not because whatever emotion comes forth from our bodies will stir us in a way that nothing else can do.

> **To experience emotions is to be passionate, to be hot, to really be on fire as an immortal body.**

Sometimes our expressions may sound awful. But it's just the way that person is feeling at the moment. It's important for that person to be able to express what they are feeling, even if it may seem to have a negative effect on someone else. Sometimes anger is the greatest thing that can be expressed — get it out, say it!

As immortals, we must realize that we will be constantly affecting each other, in all sorts of ways. That is part of our aliveness together! To experience emotions is to be passionate, to be hot, to really be on fire as an immortal body. That's what attracts us to one another.

That's why I like it all. I like the good emotions; I like what are considered the bad emotions. I like the restful emotions, the serenity that we can feel together, and I love when we stir the hell out of one another!

I don't want to do away with any of it. I want us to experience it all together. That's what brings about a wholeness to our living.

I love taking each other just as we are. Anything that may not seem complimentary at that moment, we will outlive with each other. But if we can't open up and share everything we feel, then that's never going to happen. So, you have to be willing to experience the consequences of what it means to really open up and to really live. When a person does, it's tremendous.

— *Bernadeane*

*A*liveness is something we are not used to on this planet. You're not supposed to really be alive here. It's kind of ironic. It's a place for human beings to live, but we're not really supposed to be alive. We haven't made it a safe place to be alive.

We cram our emotions because we're afraid we might get too alive, we might get too far out there. And so often if you're too far out there, you may feel like all of the eyes are on you. You're out there and you are in the spotlight. It is not always comfortable, because you're going to get a lot of feedback from people, both positive and negative. Some will want to join you in your aliveness, while others will want to pull you down to their level of deadness.

The reality is you can't get too emotional! You can't feel too much! You can't get too alive!

That is what happens so often when people begin to really turn for aliveness. All of a sudden they find out they've got a lot of people watching them and people around them are noticing differences in their body.

The tendency is to pull back into the old place you were in before so you won't be so noticeable. Well, I want to encourage you to get noticeable. The reality is you can't get too emotional! You can't feel too much. You can't get too alive.

The main thing is we never take thought with each other of our aliveness. We must be constantly venturing out there, not afraid to make fools of ourselves, not afraid to show all of the feelings in our bodies, no matter how we might appear to some.

Some people might say "you're too loud," or "you're too soft," or you're too this or too that. You must ignore them. You can't be constantly checking yourself to make sure you're acceptable to somebody. Immediately when you move that way you are killing yourself and the

Never pull back from your aliveness. Keep standing up and let people notice you!

rest of the bodies on the planet. You are feeding them and their death by twisting yourself in some way to be acceptable.

Remember that, if somebody is moving out of a consciousness of mortality, you're never going to please them totally. At one moment you might be too loud for them and the next moment you might be too soft. You're never going to satisfy anyone who is programmed to die, because they are not receiving their own bodies, and they're never going to receive your body just as it is.

So never pull back from your aliveness. Keep standing up and let people notice you.

— *James Russell*

10

Intimacy

U ntil now, mankind has always lived in a world where he has felt torn between two irreconcilable alternatives. On the one hand, his deepest need has always been for love, fellowship, and intimacy. On the other hand, though, he has felt powerless to secure any of these for himself in the face of certain death.

The result has been a crazy denial of reality. Man has told himself death is not real, that it is followed by life after death, that it is merely a transition to a better place, a higher realm. He has also denied the sweetness of intimacy, again in an attempt to take the sting out of death. Worst of all, he has tried to assuage his feelings of powerlessness by joining forces with death. As the old saying goes, "If you can't beat 'em, join 'em." It is in this way that man, who should be, each to one another, his own greatest boon, has instead seemingly become his own worst enemy.

This is why mankind seems to fear intimacy so. It is not that he is afraid of intimacy itself, but that intimacy infallibly brings up all his fears of loss and feelings of powerlessness which he has tried so hard to deny.

Given this situation, it is not surprising mankind has generally not been able to experience much intimacy. Even family members

Being intimate with one another is the bravest thing we can do.

have not been able to be all they are with each other, have not been willing to share their deepest experiences with one another.

And so man has continued to run from himself. It has literally been easier for people to kill each other than to be intimate.

You can see then why we say, as long as the intelligence of death rules, there is never going to be peace on this planet. It doesn't matter how many great peace treaties are written or how many great men are behind the peace movement. As long as the intelligence of death rules, there never will be total peace. Mortal man always carries with him that fear and knowledge that he is going to lose another. And so, he never risks getting really close because he cannot stand the pain of separation.

That's why we say that being intimate with one another is the bravest thing we can do.

The irony of man's fears is, lack of intimacy is helping the process of death. In running from each other we are killing ourselves. Death is not just that final expiration of life, it is the entire process leading up to that moment. Until we end all forms of separation, death is something that is working in our bodies on a constant basis. The grave is just the end result of the death that operates in bodies. The real death is separation, the lack of intimacy of our bodies together.

What is immortal intimacy like? There are many answers to this, none of them complete.

First of all, physical immortality is the deepest intimacy that anyone will ever have, because immortality frees us from the fear of separation.

At the same time, intimacy is the reason for our immortality. We cannot even think of being on this planet forever without having intimacy between us. Life as lone identities has no meaning.

There is a glorious release in intimacy, the feeling that all the barriers are crumbling, that we are becoming vulnerable and open to other bodies on the planet.

There is also an immortal respect which comes from acknowledging we are together forever.

Because of respect, we don't abuse each other, we are not presumptuous, we don't take advantage of one another.

We respect each other for the individuality of our different forms. At the same time, though, we are conscious of the biological connection between us. We recognize that we are different parts making up a whole — different organs that together make up a total organism. As a result, we do not envy each other our abilities, for they all contribute to the whole, which we all are.

Out of this respect, we dare to recognize one another even as ourselves. We dare even to speak, to move, to keep that person's life, to cause them to be aware of what may be destroying them.

I ntimacy is often equated with sex. However, to be intimate does not mean that we have to go to bed with one another.

At the same time, though, immortal intimacy is a very physical, even sensual, experience. After all, being physical is what we're all about as immortals. We're body, we're substance. We're that which you can handle, touch, feel, talk to, listen to and receive from.

Sensuality is the aliveness of our physical senses. When we are intimate, all of our senses are touched so deeply with one another that we are excited, we are drawn to one another. We are turned on by each other's presence, our aliveness, our touch. We experience a total sensuality and sexuality with one another.

We cannot be afraid of any of these feelings for one another. We cannot pull back from one another because we are afraid to feel. All of our true feelings for each other are healthy and expand our aliveness with each other.

We need not act on all our feelings, though. Because we are willing to feel everything with one another does not mean that we engage in promiscuity. As immortals, we are in tune

> **We cannot pull back from one another because we are afraid to feel.**

with ourselves and are aware, alert and responsible for our actions. And because we do not deny our most intimate feelings, promiscuous sex is not even a temptation. We find that it is intimacy we crave, not sex.

Once one gets used to intimacy, to have anything less with someone becomes almost unbearable. That is why we are building an immortal society where we can feel the comfortableness of being at home with one another. If we can get comfortable with one another then perhaps we can begin to feel truly at home on the planet.

☆ ☆ ☆ ☆ ☆

T here is a cellular intimacy, a feeling as though I could walk right into you. I am at home when I am with you. You are my eternal home.

Even though I am Charles Paul Brown and it appears that I am a separate entity from you, because of our immortal kinship, we experience that familiarity, the likeness, the biological sameness. This intimacy comes from a recognition that we are of the same immortal species. I feel

> **I feel as if I can walk right in, sit right down and make myself at home in the cells and atoms of your body.**

as if I can walk right in, sit right down and make myself at home in the cells and atoms of your body.

— Charlie Paul

☆ ☆ ☆ ☆ ☆

*I*ntimacy, to me, is when we are so fused in one another that we have no other place to go but to one another. We make each other more important than any land we own — we're not willing to kill each other over any land. We end the geographical boundaries because we end the biological ones in our bodies.

> ## Intimacy, to me, is when we are so fused in one another that we have no other place to go but to one another.

In our intimacy, we go for a depth of communication with each other that exceeds any of those boundaries. We take up the courage to go past those fears. That's immortal intimacy.

— *James Russell*

11

Cellular Intercourse

C ellular intercourse is an exchange of energy between immortal bodies that takes place at a cellular level. When this happens, our words and our energy, the vibration of what we are as immortal flesh, is juicing the cells of each other's bodies.

Up until now, intercourse has been limited to specific parts of the body, focusing on the mind, or on the pelvic region. But cellular intercourse involves all the cells in the body. Out of that manifestation, out of that fusion, there is a magnificent form of life that is produced from our bodies experiencing an exchange of energy. There is a sparking of one another, whether it be through our words, our touch, or the energy which is released from us. If one could see microscopically, there is a physical exchange of energy which nurtures the whole body. This is what we call the cellular intercourse.

Before there can be a cellular intercourse there must first be a cellular awakening. When there isn't the aliveness in the cells of the body, the awakening, there cannot be the intercourse that is really the consummation of the embracing of our bodies. When there is an awakening

> *There is a physical exchange of energy which nurtures the whole body.*

of the cells of our bodies, the communication and the intercourse is unlimited.

To experience cellular intercourse, you have to experience more than yourself. You have to come in contact with another immortal body. In making contact with another immortal person, there is an intercourse which takes place bringing about a stimulation and, in turn, producing a freshness of the body, a newness of one's form. The number of people involved does not matter — it could be one other person, or an auditorium full of 500 people — but it takes more than just the individual to experience cellular intercourse.

Without there being a cellular intercourse, our experience has been that it is difficult to maintain an ongoing sexual relationship. People often say, when you really have someone you love, your sexual relationship just keeps getting better and better all of the time. But we have seen, so often, when people don't have the aliveness of each other's bodies, their physical love making doesn't get any better. In fact, they tend to not have it. They then seek others to have this stimulation with, and they end up leaving each other because they are not having the aliveness of their bodies together. We have found, without that awakening in a relationship, the relationship will die because you're not having this aliveness with each other. No matter, mentally, how much you want to be together or think you want to be together, if you're not having the aliveness with each other, you will part.

When a couple is experiencing a cellular intercourse, though, their sexual pleasure with each other is enhanced tremendously. Because we are quick with each other's bodies and we're always stirring that aliveness, our intercourse with each other gets better and better. Having a cellular intercourse brings us into a potency when we do have sexual intercourse, so that the whole body experiences it rather than just the pelvic area. It is healing, it is nurturing, it is a release, an exchange of energy. That's what it is when you experience an orgasm, it's the body itself releasing energy. The energy, then, is the spark of life. Within is the sperm, the seed. When two bodies flow together, it's the body's release that brings new life into being.

☆ ☆ ☆ ☆ ☆

*T*his is what is happening to us as immortals. We're quickening the cells of our bodies, making them alive, and we experience a deeper and deeper communication with each other. It never ceases to amaze me. Each day I say, "Can it get any greater? Can there be more?" Only to find the next moment we are going to deeper levels with each other. This is what makes it so stimulating, exciting and wonderful.

What I have observed is, we are experiencing a constant renewing of our intercourse and excitement with each other, and our aliveness is getting

It's exciting to think about days a thousand years from now together.

greater every day. This is the bond which keeps us responding to each other more and more all of the time. The stimulation from this reality keeps us alive and wanting to be with each other more. We look forward to the next day and the aliveness we share together.

It's important to be excited about one's aliveness today. It's also a wonderful feeling to wake up each morning with an excitement about the day itself but most of all one another. It's exciting to think about days *a thousand years from now together, to feel the bright-ness of how much more exciting it gets to be with each other.*

— James Russell

☆ ☆ ☆ ☆ ☆

*T*he mind has always been seeking to learn the truth, ever learning and never coming to the truth. This mental truth is always evasive. The mind has been programmed to operate in symbols. So, it wants word symbols to teach the mind how to respond, how to become something, whereas the cells begin to respond innately and do not have to learn to be immortal. Instead, there is a cellular awakening from the cellular intercourse which begins to take place.*

The immortal cells have been dormant in our bodies. They have waited for the bridegroom to come. They have made themselves ready to sound, ready to receive the penetration of the energy of their immortality. That is the bridegroom that comes to the waiting cells of the body.

— Charles Paul

12

Immortal Sexuality

I n the last few decades we have seen tremendous strides in the area of human sexuality. It's wonderful in what began to happen in the expanding freedom of sexuality, releasing outdated moral and ethical codes that had been imposed by a very religious society. As man began to awaken to a freedom of sexuality, this was a very beautiful step in man's aliveness because it was bringing him closer to his body. He was beginning to accept there was nothing wrong with his sexual responses.

This acceptance of our sexuality is absolutely essential for immortal bodies. The condemnation of the sexual act, or any feeling that sex is dirty, is simply a reflection of a deeper feeling that the body itself is unclean, base or unworthy. It is feelings like these which have caused man to reject his body, and to die, in search of a sanitary, sterile afterlife.

It's a beautiful experience to have physical intercourse with each other. Love making is wonderful, and we would never do or say anything to discredit the beauty of this experience.

At the same time, sexual freedom has not been enough. Sex in itself has still blocked man. He's gotten lost in it. It's been such a limited

Sexual freedom has not been enough.

way to have a closeness with one another. It's been a distraction at times, keeping him from taking the next step into the cells and atoms of one another's bodies. It's often been used as a means of keeping a relationship superficial, of avoiding any real depths. It's kept us from having in-depth fusion and cellular intercourse with each other.

Immortal bodies have to take sexuality even further. The cellular intercourse we've spoken of previously becomes the forerunner to the total immortal sexuality which begins to be released from the body. Then, upon a body experiencing a sexual release, there is a rush, a total releasing of every cell and atom to be free. When you have this, then your love making far exceeds what you thought it could be. Until the body is accepted as being physically immortal, this immortal sexual energy is held within the body and only released at intervals because the body is still temporary, and sex is still a temporal experience, wrapped up in the life-death cycle.

The total freedom of immortal sexuality is something new. Certain religious circles have sought, at times, to take sex into a sacredness, but the body was always considered a vessel or temple to house the spirit. Even if they experienced a certain high, they still took it into a religious experience. Even if it was released from the lower spine and came up through the body and rushed through the head, all of this was beautiful, but it was still seemingly tapping into God as the unknown source of our aliveness.

I n immortal sexuality there is an androgyny that takes place within the body such that we are both male and female. Nature has produced this condition, so the male and female are within all of our bodies, but there must be a balance which brings about the distinctly immortal form.

In the world of discrimination and judgment, there has been the practice of categorizing the heterosexual, the bisexual, the homosexual and of course the asexual, where there is no sexual feeling at all, no sexual identification.

But, we are aware, in being immortal, that there is an androgyny of us that leaves no room for discrimination. We respond to the cellular intercourse between humans, whether they be male or female, no matter what their sexual preference.

Physical immortality does not leave any room for promiscuity. Today, one-night stands are becoming less common. A lot of people say, "Well, this is because of AIDS, etc." That may be true, to a certain extent. But, there is also a sense of feeling in bodies that have had one-night stands and felt someone come close to them — it is too painful to condition themselves after the one-night stand is over. They felt something, and yet they feel lonely and isolated the next day. They got their rocks off with one another and are left feeling empty. People today are wanting something more intimate, more lasting.

> *Physical immortality does not leave any room for promiscuity.*

For immortals to be promiscuous, once there is the cellular awakening, is impossible, because there is an intimacy of receiving one another into the cells of the body so that you are not just ships passing in the night.

When we speak of promiscuity, we're speaking of when you suddenly find an attraction to someone, a beautiful form or body. But unless there is a receiving back from that person the signals of an immortal language and intelligence, the immortal body does not respond. No matter how beautiful that person is, the body does not respond because the response is unto the like cell that is also immortal.

Beyond this, we have no moral standards to lay down to someone as far as their sexual preference, as far as their choice of who they would live with, or with how many they would want to live. Even if there would be a multiple living, there still would not be the promiscuity or a using of bodies for one's own self-gratification.

This is what we're about. What we are out to do is create relationships on every level. We must create intimate relationships so deep and satisfying one doesn't have to go out and have affairs and play around with each other. At the same time, there is a feeling of safety to enjoy other bodies on a very deep level and not get lost in the sexuality.

☆ ☆ ☆ ☆ ☆

*T*o me, androgyny has to do with Jesus. In one sense, he was neither male nor female: he was a male body but, being neither male nor female, he was experiencing androgyny to where he could not discriminate. His response was both unto the male and the female. That's why his passion could touch all who came to him and felt that passion of love. This is what emanated from his body.

To be immortal is to be of that same nature. We respond on a cellular level to bodies and not because of gender. The quality of response we receive from those forms is what we experience, not their maleness or femaleness.

— Charles Paul

13

Diet and Nutrition

Physical immortality can never be obtained solely by means of diet and nutrition. That is to say, there is no "perfect" diet that can guarantee immortality.

At the same time, though, nutrition and the food we eat and what we take into our bodies is very important. These factors can make a vital difference in the quality of our living. To be fully alive, we must be able to enjoy, utilize and experience our bodies to the fullest.

There is no single diet or regimen that is right for everyone. What we want to convey is not some law of nutrition but for each one of us to be in touch with what is good for us. We all have that consciousness in our own beings. Already in the cells of your body you know what is right for you but you may have lost contact with it. We want to stimulate you to get in contact with that cellular knowledge, to really move and be alive!

There are all kinds of programs available in diet, nutrition, exercise and related areas but people often don't benefit from these programs as much as they could because they don't get in touch with themselves and what is good for their own bodies. Each person is a unique individual in this sense. What one person can eat, another person may not be able to.

We all know what to do. We all know, when we are in touch with our bodies, how to eat, what to do for our own individual form, and what is good for us. We know when we are eating too much. We know when we are overweight. When we experience a cellular awakening even our taste buds become acutely sensitized as to what we should have.

This is not to say, however, that we have nothing to offer each other in this area. Keep in mind that your individual self is not the whole. You may hear from or about yourself by way of another person. You may not be totally clear about what you should do for your physical body. Because you are part of a larger whole you can receive from others around you who may have the answer that you cannot find for yourself.

At the same time you may experience for individuals who are your life, some things they should do for their bodies. You may know, where they don't know consciously, what to do. In that case, you are responsible to express to them what you really feel concerning them. Then, you are to let go.

We are to express, we're to move, we're to encourage others to move in that which will profit them. We need to be that stimulus for others to get in touch with their

> *We are to express, we're to move, we're to encourage others to move in that which will profit them.*

own bodies. But then they are responsible for taking what we have given them and putting it into physical manifestation. We cannot do that for them. Each person has to put into physical manifestation that which is real for them, for their life.

This is where we are powerless. We are both powerful and powerless. We are powerful in being all we are to one another but we are powerless in living each other's life. It's simply not possible.

We cannot struggle to make another person do what we feel is best for him or her. That is a struggle unto death.

We cannot fall into the trap of laying down rules for each other. We always seem to set up rules only for them to be broken. Then we end up using those rules against each other.

For example, we say, "Oh, that person didn't quit smoking. He didn't mind what I said. He is not paying attention to me. I won't give him the time of day anymore." We end up turning on, or from, that person.

There is an important distinction here. It is very important for us to always express ourselves. It's important to let others know our feelings about them. It's very important for us to express all of what we feel with each other and what we desire of a healthiness with each other.

On the other hand, it's important not to make it a law if they don't respond to us — if they don't quit smoking, for example. We cannot use that as an excuse to turn from them. We cannot impose our feelings on them.

We're getting into dangerous ground when we try to say what's really going to make you live the best, and what's not going to make you live the best. We find ourselves saying what is going to make you immortal and what is not. Then we have an excuse to divide ourselves, because you're not immortal.

This pattern of division is so subtle, it runs so deep. All of the time, in each of us, things come up that would want to separate us. It's only with the cellular connection we have made with each other that we are able to combat that chemistry of separation.

☆ ☆ ☆ ☆ ☆

I *want to be able to enjoy climbing the mountain if I want to. I want to be able to climb a set of stairs without running out of breath. I want to be able to walk the street, ride a bike, and feel the healthiness of my body. This is what living is all about.*

I also want to be able to experience you, without letting sickness or poor health get in our way. So many times sickness separates people. They are too sick to come to a meeting. They aren't feeling well enough to communicate. They are feeling too poorly to really get into the depths of things. They are too bogged down in their body cellularly—perhaps they ate too much for lunch that day and they can't really feel themselves. I don't want any of this to rob me of you.

I want to be able to experience you, without letting sickness or poor health get in our way.

— James Russell

☆ ☆ ☆ ☆ ☆

I have come to the place now that it is almost impossible for me to eat red meat. I will not say, about anything, that I will never do it again; but, for me, for now, something inside me recoils even from the thought of red meat.

I didn't think this would ever be. I used to love cheeseburgers. I absolutely had to have one once in a while. The last time I tried to have a cheeseburger, I thought it was going to be great, because I'd been craving it. Instead, it was repulsive to me. It just didn't taste well at all.

Someone wrote us from England concerning diet and nutrition and being a vegetarian. I do know that I feel lighter when I'm eating just vegetables and fresh fruits. However, I have also felt, concerning fish and fowl, that they are sometimes helpful in providing a grounding for us. Somehow, for me, a totally vegetarian diet seems to produce a feeling of a split within the body. I feel that certain life forms have been put here to serve our bodies, and fish and fowl may be among these.

I knew an individual who was a total vegetarian for fifteen years and his health was failing. I was feeling that his body was lacking in some sort of protein that he could only get from meat. Sure enough, he went to see Ramtha and Ramtha said he needed to start eating meat.

I, or anyone else, could have said that to him, and he would have ignored us. He wouldn't have eaten meat for anyone. But, a 50,000 year old spiritual entity caused him to start eating meat.

— *Charles Paul*

☆ ☆ ☆ ☆ ☆

*I*f smoking is bad for you, then I have to trust that you will know it. I won't shove it down your throat, so that you don't even want to be around me after a while.

Whether you are smoking, drinking, or whatever, I'm going to give my greatest enjoyment of you. I'm not here on this planet to condemn you or to struggle with you. I'm here to have fun with you and enjoy you.

I'm not here on this planet to condemn you or to struggle with you. I'm here to have fun with you and enjoy you.

I think that man has always created laws because he wasn't in touch with his body to really be able to have that flow. He's always been separated from his flesh, from one another. Our species is not of the law of nature anymore.

— *James Russell*

☆ ☆ ☆ ☆ ☆

*L*aw will always bring about a condemnation. Anything that is legislated will always shorten life.

This was the very principle illustrated in the old testament during Moses' time. There was more to the story of Israel than just being delivered from Egyptian bondage. There were 5,000,000 who came up out of bondage. They were to experience physical immortality. Their clothes didn't wear out, their shoes didn't wear out. They experienced this aliveness that was emanating from their physical bodies.

Moses then thought he could legislate this condition. So, he brought forth the Ten Commandments, which were on the tablets of stone. The law shortened people's lives. At that time, people lived to be much older, some to 200, 300 years of age, at least 120 — they considered 120 nothing.

But the ten commandments shortened the life span to three score and ten, or seventy, years.

So, this expresses to me, again, that the aliveness and immortality is to come forth from within the seed itself, from within the cell.

Anything that is legislated will always shorten life.

This is why, after giving Moses the commandments, God said that the next time he would write his laws upon the fleshly tablets of the heart.

That, to me, is writing it, awakening the cells of the body to where it is the changing of the DNA. There is a new law: not the law of death that has decreed that man is evolving through the aging process unto death; rather there is a new law that is unto everlasting life, that begins to manifest internally from the cells of the body.

There is a new law that is unto everlasting life, that begins to manifest itself internally from the cells of the body.

— *Charles Paul*

14

Prosperity

P hysical immortality requires us to look at prosperity in a different way. As with so many other areas, it causes us to reexamine our old attitudes, and inspires fresh approaches.

Our whole concept of prosperity today has been created from a death consciousness, a survival consciousness. The result is a greed so strong a person can never get enough money, can never get enough security. The greed is birthed from the consciousness of death. A person thinks he may die if he doesn't have enough money, so he begins to associate money with life, and can never get enough. Eventually a person like this is simply racing to grab whatever he can.

The reason why he can never get enough, of course, is that all the time he is scrambling after more money, he is starving for his real life. As long as there is worry and concern about survival, that person is a servant of money, and can never walk free.

We are all familiar with the story, told time and time again, of the person who says "I have all this money, but I still haven't found happiness." They have a lot of money, but they aren't alive with it: they still can't shake that feeling of poverty. It doesn't matter how much money they have, they are always either worried about losing what they have, or always struggling to have more.

No matter how much money some people have, they are always either worried about losing it or struggling to have more.

Another fallacy in our thinking about prosperity has been the idea that we can achieve some form of immortality by passing money on to our heirs. A person thinks he's going to die sometime so he races to get everything he can for posterity.

It's funny, people pile all this money up and it begins to have a life of its own. They're so sure that they have to die, but they think the money they've accumulated can live on. They begin to seek some sort of life after death by associating themselves with their fortune: they leave it to their children; they have a public building constructed with it, and get their name on it; perhaps they establish a philanthropic fund to preserve their name. Whatever the means, this just becomes one more excuse to amass even more money, and the cycle continues, and they die even faster.

Through it all, mortal man looks at prosperity as something that comes to him externally, just because his karma is right or because he has been able to manipulate the right deal.

P hysical immortality changes all our ideas about prosperity. In awakening to being immortal we begin to feel and sense prosperity from a different level altogether.

Immortality enables us to get off the wheel of survival. We are no longer worried about whether or not we are going to survive, and so we lose that fear, that sense of desperation about money. There is a relaxation which takes place in the body.

At the same time, we lose the chemistry of greed, a scarcity consciousness, or a dog-eat-dog attitude. We give up any feeling others have to die in order for us to live. We lose all our excuses to allow any human being to starve on this planet. The greed is over. The robbing of one another is over.

This doesn't mean everyone will have the same level of finances, in some socialistic concept. We cannot force prosperity on anyone. But there shouldn't be any person starving, no matter what race they come from, no matter what part of the world, no matter what the differences have been or whether they are so-called enemies or not. There is food enough for everybody.

Immortals recognize that we *are* our prosperity: all other forms of prosperity start with us. Money is not prosperity: physically immortal prosperity is Bernadeane. Being prosperous has to do with the cellular aliveness that we experience. Prosperity is chemical. It's what is going on chemically within our bodies in the sense of what we feel ourselves to be. Being prosperous is experiencing no limitations.

> ***Immortality enables us to get off the wheel of survival.***

The more we experience being physically prosperous, the more we will cause prosperity all the way around. This is where we end all the struggles. As we prosper in our bodies, we prosper in every way.

Because of our aliveness together, we draw all forms or prosperity unto us; we're inheriting the earth. This is a part of the same principle of moving out of the anointing of our bodies, rather than struggling. It's not moving from might or by power, but the essence of what we are together.

Immortal prosperity also has to do with the giving of oneself. There are many ways to give of oneself. As immortals we realize, since we are without limit, we can give of ourselves without limit. This frees us to give without worrying about running out. The more physically prosperous we are, the more we feel we have to share with others.

Of course, it's not a one-way street. Immortals not only give of themselves, they receive from others who are their very self. For immortals, both giving and receiving become glorious and wonderful experiences.

Paradoxically, when we finally realize that money is not the source of our happiness, it then frees us to really enjoy money. It becomes just a greater manifestation of an enjoyment of all of our lives together. We look on it as an enhancement of the quality of our being immortal. It frees us to be able to move about without any feeling of confinement. It brings a freedom of movement that adds to our enjoyment of our immortality. We love the best and the quality that compliments us.

We need to begin to recognize our inheritance and begin to draw to us that which we already are. We deserve it. Money is to serve us. All these things are to serve our bodies.

But it all starts with knowing that whether I have any of those things or not, I'm alive with you. Out of that feeling, we never do without.

☆ ☆ ☆ ☆ ☆

*M*oney is flesh. Money looks like the green stuff, but it is flesh. It doesn't happen without the body. There is no manifestation of money except that a person brings it about.

— *Bernadeane*

☆ ☆ ☆ ☆ ☆

*R*etiring sounds so awful. It's just a way of dying. Retiring is a way of ending one's life. The amazing thing is our system has it set up that after being here 65 years on the planet, you're to retire. My God, a person hasn't even reached their first 100 years yet and they already have them dead!

— *Bernadeane*

☆ ☆ ☆ ☆ ☆

*M*an has created the whole thing. Man has created his limitations; man has created his prosperity. Man does it all. We're realizing more and more every day how potent and how great mankind really is — all the more so once we awaken to the realization that death was never a requirement for us.

— *Bernadeane*

☆ ☆ ☆ ☆ ☆

We are the most prosperous bodies on the face of the Earth. We have one another. The greatest wealth that we can have is one another's flesh. Out of that, we're not moving in the survival chemistry anymore.

What's different about us is we aren't out there trying to beat the pavement to bring forth a living. We're not fighting against one another or competing with one another. There is a moving out of an aliveness of each

> ## We are the most prosperous bodies on the face of the earth. We have one another.

other rather than trying to survive to stay alive. We're moving out of this aliveness that draws to us all the prosperity.

The difference in what we're creating now is our aliveness with each other: then our prosperity is already there. We don't have to go out and find it; it's an inheritance. We're not searching all over for the substance of our life. We have the substance and out of that we draw all the wealth of the world, all of the money we need.

It's energy. When you're moving from that energy all things are yours.

— *James Russell*

15

Beyond Belief Systems

P hysical immortality is more than just a belief system. Some people, when they first hear us, say "oh, that's just your belief", or "you're just practicing positive thinking." This is not what we are about at all.

Man has put his faith in untold numbers of different belief systems, and they have always failed him. They have always led to death.

We are not interested in developing a new belief system; we're not interested in promoting a new philosophy; we're not interested in starting a new religion — we're not out to impart some great truth.

Nothing you have read in this book will make you physically immortal, no matter how strongly you may believe what you have read. Belief is not capable of making anyone immortal.

A belief is something that can be accepted or rejected, that you can be convinced of, or dissuaded from, that can be the subject of argument. We're not interested in any of this.

Our images of the mind and the body and the relationship between them have been of the mind being the superior power, being in control, and the body doing the bidding of the mind. The latest scientific research is showing, however,

> *Physical immortality is not a truth you can believe or disbelieve — it is something you awaken to.*

that the mind and the rest of the body are so intertwined that they cannot say which, if either, is in control.

Many people today are beginning to realize the power of the mind, the power of affirmations, the power of belief. The mind is powerful, but the power of the mind is nothing compared to the power of the whole body. The power of a belief held only in the mind is nothing compared to the power of a cellular passion felt throughout the whole body.

Physical immortality is not a truth that you can believe or disbelieve — it is something you awaken to. It is something you feel from within that is more powerful than anything you have ever felt — you feel it in every cell of your body. It is your awakening to yourself, your true identity. Physical immortality is your very substance — it is you.

Being physically immortal is the body, it's not a religion. Religion comes out from man. Religion is something that man has created for himself to live by. One can't create physical immortality to live by, it's already the body. What has been taking place is we are awakening to who we have always been.

Once you awaken to your true nature, you can no more deny it than you can deny your own heartbeat. Once you awaken to physical immortality, you can no more give it up than you can give up breathing.

☆ ☆ ☆ ☆ ☆

*W*e are not moving on this planet to bring about a new truth or new religion. My feeling is that the world is bored with religion. People are in a sleep and a belief with it. They're not coming forth in the aliveness of what the belief is all about to begin with.

The difference between a belief system, or a religion, or a philosophy, and what we are, is just being ourselves. The bottom line is our bodies. When everything else is said and done, when all the words have been expressed, it's just us.

What we're bringing to the world is one another. It's physical. We're not bringing a new belief that could be agreed upon or disagreed upon. We are bringing ourselves.

We just come as ourselves, naked. We're not trying to be received or rejected, it's what we are.

You could say all of the beautiful words in the world and make all the big presentations, but when it really comes down to it, we're left with the question, "What are we going to do with each other on this planet?"

That goes beyond the message of any belief system. It brings it down to each other. Then it's not a belief system we're talking about, it's physical bodies.

This is the only question we're interested in answering. After all the belief systems are said and done, where are we with each other?

—James Russell

☆ ☆ ☆ ☆ ☆

I could go on and on about the great philosophers that have lived. *Much truth has been expounded by these philosophers that I'm very thankful for,* but their truth is always about something. Whereas, in being physically immortal, it is physically who and what I am, biologically and psychologically.

Physical immortality is not something I try to learn about. It comes forth from me when I meditate because it's what I am cellularly.

I'm not trying to learn externally to be a certain way in order to fit some principle of some belief system or doctrine. The belief system is a perpetual learning. It always keeps you from being able to experience the reality of yourself.

To be physically immortal is what I am and it's coming from within the cells of my body. I'm not trying to learn, yet I'm ever expanding.

What I'm experiencing in the cells of my own body is that hunger, that thirst to wake up to who and what I really am.

Immortality is nothing but a belief system without there being a cellular awakening. This reality is the difference in being immortal and being an immortalist. An immortalist is one who plays with being immortal. An immortal has no choice: he has felt that awakening, and knows who he is.

An immortal has no choice: he has felt that awakening and knows who he is.

— Charles Paul

16

About the Authors

C harles Paul Brown, Bernadeane and James Russell Strole are internationally recognized speakers on the subject of physical immortality. They have been speaking and writing on this exciting topic since 1960. Their desire to awaken immortality in others has taken them on numerous speaking tours throughout the United States, as well as around the globe to countries such as Australia, Austria, Belgium, England, France, Germany, Holland, Ireland, Israel, New Zealand and Venezuela, to name just a few. Wherever they have appeared, they have found those who have responded to their cellular aliveness, and they are now in constant, growing demand for international speaking engagements.

The workshops given by these three are unique and exciting events. Each one is always different, since CBJ, as they are known, have no fixed format for their appearances. Their expressions are always spontaneous and deeply felt. Their events generally include time for expressions from other participants in the event as well. These three do more than just speak: they give themselves completely in the aliveness of each moment.

CBJ also make frequent appearances in national and international media. They are often subjects of newspaper and magazine articles, television documentaries, and are popular guests on radio and television talk shows.

> *These three do more than just speak: they give themselves completely in the aliveness of each moment.*

C harles Paul awakened to physical immortality in 1960. Prior to that turning point in his life, he had served in the Air Force, become an accomplished nightclub entertainer, and later worked as a men's fashion buyer for major department stores in California. At the time of his awakening to immortality, he was an ordained Christian minister. He met Bernadeane in 1961, and they have been together since 1962.

Beginning in 1960, Charles Paul realized that man was living far below his true potential, and that physical immortality was his true birthright. The next eleven years were spent in extensive travel throughout the United States speaking to religious and metaphysical groups. Filled with the excitement of being totally alive, he hoped to awaken many others to their own true state of being.

In 1966, Charles Paul began to author a newsletter called "The Eternal Flame." Many of these writings have been collected into two booklets, entitled "Physical Immortality," volumes I and II.

In 1971, Charles Paul and Bernadeane realized that their next step was to bring together others who felt as they did in a single location, and it was then that they established the Flame Foundation in Scottsdale, Arizona. Many who had been touched by them in their travels soon joined them there, and this body of people has continued to grow since then.

Over the years, Charles Paul has remained constant in his hunger for others to bond with him in a deathless living. He continues to sound the call to others with a clarity and passion that is his alone. His voice is the "deep that calls unto the deep," awakening all who will hear to a new potential for humankind.

Bernadeane was born in Salem, Oregon. She too was awakening to an experience of physical immortality, even before her meeting with Charles Paul. After her meeting, she underwent a change which transcended anything she had experienced as a child and young adult in the church.

It was only after many years of traveling with Charles Paul that Bernadeane began to publicly express her own thoughts and feeling about immortality. Since then, she has revealed herself to be an articulate and passionate spokesperson for immortality in her own right. She has truly found her own unique voice, and her expressions on immortality are as personal and direct as she is herself.

Bernadeane, a former model, is also a vocalist, an accomplished musician on the piano and organ, and composer of a number of songs that express her feelings about immortal living.

Those who know her well have often compared Bernadeane to a laser beam: direct, intense and powerful. She makes a strong impact on everyone she meets. She seems to always move from the very core of her being, with a sureness that comes from trusting her innermost feelings.

Charles Paul and Bernadeane have children, Kevin Brown and Kim Brown, who are themselves integral parts of the Foundation in Scottsdale. They and their families have joined with Charles and Bernadeane in an immortal connection.

J ames Russell was born in Arizona. He is a graduate of Phoenix College, where he participated in football and other sports. His extracurricular activities there also included membership in the United Nations Club and other humanitarian pursuits.

After exploring several different traditional Christian religions, James studied Integral Yoga as taught by Sri Aurobindo. These studies introduced him to the concept of physical immortality.

When he met Charles Paul and Bernadeane in 1968, James knew that he had found his own. Since then, he has worked continuously with them to build the community in Scottsdale, and to spread immortality around the globe.

James is known for his quick sense of humor. He balances this with a passion, a gentleness and a heartfelt warmth that know no limits. His unending stirring is for people to make each other's lives a daily "heaven on earth."

Together, CBJ form a totality that is more than the sum of their individual contributions. Each is a unique individual, distinct in appearance, personality and expression. They are united as one, however, in their passion for humankind to live free from death, in a world of unlimited aliveness.

T hese three are founders of the Flame Foundation, an organization established to help awaken others to physical immortality. The foundation holds meetings twice a week in Scottsdale, Arizona, providing a forum for people to come together for a celebration of their aliveness, and for their expansion as a cellular body. It is in these meetings, as well as in the daily living with each other, that CBJ and others take immortality beyond a mental concept and into a deep physical reality.

Meetings generally consist of spontaneous expressions by one person at a time. A microphone is available for that purpose and the microphone is generally open to anyone attending the meeting, for at least a portion of every gathering. Some members sing, and piano accompaniment is usually available. The most popular subject at the meetings, of course, is physical immortality. The nature of the expressions is constantly varying, however, as the people there continually go deeper in their explorations of their limitless existence together.

A large group of people regularly attend the meetings in Scottsdale. CBJ also have affiliated groups that meet regularly in other locations in the United States and around the world.

Attendees at these meetings are a diverse group. Many have come from traditional Christian religious backgrounds. Others have come from the field of humanistic psychology, from contact with Eastern religions, from personal growth groups and from the "New Age" movement. People come in all ages, as well.

The group in Scottsdale functions as the "propulsion system" for CBJ, contributing their time, energy and finances to sending these three around the world in search of their own.

The Foundation publishes a quarterly magazine entitled *Forever Alive*. This contains information about upcoming events, news about global immortal happenings, and expressions by CBJ and others. Annual subscriptions are available for $25, which includes the cost of mailing your magazine to wherever you happen to live on this planet.

The Convergence is an annual event, sponsored by the Foundation, which is attended by people from all over the globe. This event is held during the summer in Scottsdale, and has grown to a full two weeks for the past two years. The 1991 event drew over 500 attendees from around the world, and featured simultaneous translation into five different languages.

Please write or call for more information. CBJ look forward to meeting you!

People Unlimited, Inc.
The Infinite Aliveness Company
15560 North Frank Lloyd Wright Blvd., Ste B-4/230
Scottsdale, Arizona 85260 USA
(602) 949-4344 or Fax: (602) 368-0998
Website: www.live4ever.com E-Mail: peoplunltd@aol.com

☆ ☆ ☆ ☆ ☆

Who are Charles Paul Brown, Bernadeane and James Russell Strole?

Although their appearance is distinctive, nothing about it marks them as radicals and revolutionaries. More than anything else, they look like movie stars: lithe and well-groomed, their clothes expensive and well-tailored, they move with a grace and assurance we are used to seeing only on the screen.

And yet, there is something immediately different about them—an animation, an aliveness, a certain flair —that makes them impossible to categorize with any certainty. Charles Paul is tall and distinguished, with a sparkle in his eye and an air of refinement. Bernadeane is small and striking, powerful and direct, a female dynamo. James Russell is tall and broad-shouldered, almost overpowering one moment in his passion and immediacy, then soft and smiling the next. Each is totally different from the other two, and yet they all somehow seem to share a common core, to have come from the same mold in some hard-to-define way.

There is something much like magic that one feels in their presence. There is a palpable connection that is felt, like an electric current joining them to everyone in the room: an attraction, an openness, a warmth that feels like sunshine. They seem to develop a personal, intimate connection with each person in the room, even in a crowd of hundreds. They have the rare ability to give themselves completely in every minute. Every word they speak, every movement, every gesture, every facial expression reveals more of who they are, and at the same time somehow encourages all around them to be more of who they are. There is a quickening and an enlivening *that one feels just by being around them. The lasting impression they inevitably leave is of the infinite worth of themselves, and of everyone else.*

To hear these three speak to a crowd is like hearing a great jazz band perform. Their improvised expressions seem to well up from somewhere deep inside them, raw and true and un-deniable. Common themes recur from time to time, but each expression is different, fresh and passionate, coming not from memory but from what they are feeling that moment. Each time they touch a subject they seem to go deeper, constantly expanding their limits, always staking out new territory.

> **Each is totally different from the other two, and yet they all somehow seem to share a common core.**

At times these three seem almost superhuman, more than mere mortals. This impression is only half-true, though: they are more than merely mortal, but they are no more than human. Rather, they are living demonstrations of what it means to be fully human, once the limitation of death is removed. They are flesh and blood and bone, like you and me, yet they make us realize that being human is enough, more than enough—in fact, all we could ever want.

— Herb Bowie

** indicates many references of these subjects throughout

ORDER FORM

Item	Price	Quantity	Total
Together Forever: An Invitation to be Physically Immortal, by CBJ	$9.95	___	$ ____
Latest Audio Cassette from CBJ's Monthly Tape Series	$10.00	___	____
20% Postage & Handling for Above Items	20%		____
Forever Alive One-Year Subscription	$25.00	___	____
CBJ Information Packet, Including a Complimentary Issue of *Forever Alive* and a Schedule of Upcoming Events	*FREE!*	___	
Total Payment Sent			$ ____

Name: _____

Address: _____

City: _____ State: _____ Zip: _____

Country: _____

All Prices and Payments in U.S. Funds, Please!

SendCheck, Money Order or Credit Card Information.

Credit Card Type: MC ☐   VISA ☐   AMEX ☐

Card Number: _____ Exp. Date: _____

Card Holder Name: _____

People Unlimited, Inc.
The Infinite Aliveness Company
15560 North Frank Lloyd Wright Blvd., Ste B-4/230
Scottsdale, Arizona 85260 USA
(602) 949-4344 or Fax: (602) 368-0998
Website: www.live4ever.com E-Mail: peoplunltd@aol.com